NEW Hymns & Worship Songs

A SUPPLEMENTARY COLLECTION

Kevin Mayhew

First published in Great Britain in 1996 by
KEVIN MAYHEW LIMITED
Rattlesden
Bury St Edmunds
Suffolk IP30 0SZ

Compilation © Kevin Mayhew Ltd 1996
Extracted from *Hymns Old & New*, New Anglican Edition

The following editions are available

Words Only	ISBN	0 86209 885 8
	Catalogue No.	1413031
Full Music (hardback)	ISBN	0 86209 886 6
	Catalogue No.	1413034

Front cover design by Veronica Ward
Printed and bound in Great Britain

Foreword

Although we hope it will be welcomed as a valuable collection in its own right, *New Hymns and Worship Songs* has a more specific purpose: to update existing Anglican hymnals so that congregations can sing the best and most loved compositions of recent years alongside the traditional hymns found in all books.

Almost 90 per cent of the nearly 300 hymns given here will not be found in either of the two most widely used Anglican hymn books: it is a great pity that congregations should be denied such standard fare as the Taizé chants, the beautiful music of Iona, Graham Kendrick's ever more popular songs or those hymns which, although widely used for many years, are not to be found in other collections, fine pieces such as *How great thou art*; *Our God reigns* and *Be still, my soul* set to the majestic tune *Finlandia*.

As well as including hymns and songs composed in recent years this collection has a small number of rewritten traditional texts. For example, *God is working his purpose out*, notoriously wayward in its metre, is given in a strictly metrical version which makes it easier to sing and, therefore, more enjoyable for all concerned. Another editorial consideration had to do with the kind of images sometimes used. There is a growing belief that, in an increasingly violent society, militarism and triumphalism should not be expressed and apparently sanctified in hymnody; the scope for misuse of those themes is frequently demonstrated. However, it must be acknowledged that some such texts have fine tunes which we should not lose, and the solution in certain cases has been to commission new texts, such as *Stand up, stand up for Jesus*; *God is our strength from days of old* and *Onward Christian pilgrims*, to fit the original tunes.

This singing of hymns and psalms in worship pre-dates Christianity. It is something that Jesus himself would have been familiar with in the temple, and he certainly sang at the Last Supper – 'After psalms had been sung they left for the Mount of Olives', writes Matthew. What a wonderful tradition we share!

We hope that in this diverse and approachable collection of hymns we have sown some seeds; that is all we can do. It is in the worship of the churches that those seeds must be brought to glorious flower.

THE PUBLISHER

1

1. A man there lived in Galilee
like none who lived before,
for he alone from first to last
our flesh unsullied wore;
a perfect life of perfect deeds
once to the world was shown,
that people all might mark his steps
and in them plant their own.

2. A man there died on Calvary
above all others brave;
the human race he saved and blessed,
himself he scorned to save.
No thought can gauge the weight
   of woe
on him, the sinless, laid;
we only know that with his blood
our ransom price was paid.

3. A man there reigns in glory now,
divine, yet human still;
that human which is all divine
death sought in vain to kill.
All pow'r is his; supreme he rules
the realms of time and space;
yet still our human cares and needs
find in his heart a place.

Somerset Corry Lowry (1855-1932)

2

*A new commandment
I give unto you:
that you love one another
as I have loved you,
that you love one another
as I have loved you.*

1. By this shall all know
that you are my disciples
if you have love one for another.
By this shall all know
that you are my disciples
if you have love one for another.

2. You are my friends
if you do what I command you.
Without my help you can do nothing.
You are my friends
if you do what I command you.
Without my help you can do nothing.

3. I am the true vine,
my Father is the gard'ner.
Abide in me: I will be with you.
I am the true vine,
my Father is the gard'ner.
Abide in me: I will be with you.

4. True love is patient,
not arrogant or boastful;
love bears all things, love is eternal.
True love is patient,
not arrogant or boastful;
love bears all things, love is eternal.

*v. 1: unknown, based on John 13:34-35
vs. 2-4: Aniceto Nazareth, based on John 15
and 1 Corinthians 13*

3

Abba, Father, let me be
yours and yours alone.
May my will for ever be
more and more your own.
Never let my heart grow cold,
never let me go.
Abba, Father, let me be
yours and yours alone.

Dave Bilbrough

4

Adoramus te, Domine.

1. With the angels and archangels:

2. With the patriarchs and prophets:

3. With the Virgin Mary,
   mother of God:

4. With the apostles and evangelists:

5. With all the martyrs of Christ:

6. With all who witness
   to the Gospel of the Lord:

7. With all your people
   of the Church throughout the world:

Taizé Community

5

1. Ah, holy Jesu,
   how hast thou offended,
   that so to judge thee
   mortals have pretended?
   By foes derided,
   by thine own rejected,
   O most afflicted.

2. Who was the guilty?
   Who brought this upon thee?
   Alas, O Lord,
   my treason hath undone thee.
   'Twas I, Lord Jesu,
   I it was denied thee:
   I crucified thee.

3. Lo, the good shepherd
   for the sheep is offered;
   the slave hath sinnèd,
   and the Son hath suffered;
   for our atonement
   Christ himself is pleading,
   still interceding.

4. For me, kind Jesu,
   was thy incarnation,
   thy mortal sorrow,
   and thy life's oblation;
   thy death of anguish
   and thy bitter passion,
   for my salvation.

5. Therefore, kind Jesu,
   since I cannot pay thee,
   I do adore thee,
   and will ever pray thee,
   think on thy pity
   and thy love unswerving,
   not my deserving.

Robert Bridges (1844-1930)
from J. Heerman (1585-1647) alt.
based on an 11th century Latin meditation

6

1. All heav'n declares
   the glory of the risen Lord.
   Who can compare
   with the beauty of the Lord?
   For ever he will be
   the Lamb upon the throne.
   I gladly bow the knee
   and worship him alone.

2. I will proclaim
   the glory of the risen Lord,
   who once was slain
   to reconcile us to God.
   For ever you will be
   the Lamb upon the throne;
   I gladly bow the knee,
   and worship you alone.

Noel and Tricia Richards
© 1987 Kingsway's Thankyou Music

7

1. All over the world
   the Spirit is moving,
   all over the world,
   as the prophets said it would be.
   All over the world
   there's a mighty revelation
   of the glory of the Lord,
   as the waters cover the sea.

2. All over this land
   the Spirit is moving,
   all over this land,
   as the prophets said it would be.
   All over this land
   there's a mighty revelation
   of the glory of the Lord,
   as the waters cover the sea.

3. All over the Church
   the Spirit is moving,
   all over the Church,
   as the prophets said it would be.
   All over the Church
   there's a mighty revelation
   of the glory of the Lord,
   as the waters cover the sea.

4. All over us all
   the Spirit is moving,
   all over us all,
   as the prophets said it would be.
   All over us all
   there's a mighty revelation
   of the glory of the Lord,
   as the waters cover the sea.

5. Deep down in my heart
   the Spirit is moving,
   deep down in my heart,
   as the prophets said it would be.
   Deep down in my heart
   there's a mighty revelation
   of the glory of the Lord,
   as the waters cover the sea.

Roy Turner (b. 1940)
© 1984 Kingsway's Thankyou Music

8

1. All that I am, all that I do,
   all that I'll ever have I offer now to you.
   Take and sanctify these gifts
   for your honour, Lord.
   Knowing that I love and serve you
   is enough reward.
   All that I am, all that I do,
   all that I'll ever have I offer now to you.

2. All that I dream, all that I pray,
   all that I'll ever make I give to you
      today.
   Take and sanctify these gifts
   for your honour, Lord.
   Knowing that I love and serve you
   is enough reward.
   All that I am, all that I do,
   all that I'll ever have I offer now to you.

Sebastian Temple (b. 1928)
© 1967 OCP Publications

9

All the nations of the earth,
praise the Lord who brings to birth
the greatest star, the smallest flow'r.
Alleluia.

1. Let the heavens praise the Lord,
   alleluia.
   Moon and stars, praise the Lord,
   alleluia.

2. Snow-capped mountains, praise
      the Lord,
   alleluia.
   Rolling hills, praise the Lord,
   alleluia.

3. Deep sea water, praise the Lord,
   alleluia.
   Gentle rain, praise the Lord,
   alleluia.

4. Roaring lion, praise the Lord,
   alleluia.
   Singing birds, praise the Lord,
   alleluia.

5. Earthly monarchs, praise the Lord,
   alleluia.
   Young and old, praise the Lord,
   alleluia.

Michael Cockett (b. 1938)

10

1. Alleluia . . .

2. Jesus is Lord . . .

3. And I love him . . .

4. Christ is risen . . .

Additional verses may be composed to suit
the occasion. For example:

5. Send your Spirit . . .

6. Abba, Father . . .

7. Come, Lord Jesus . . .

vs: 1-4 unknown, vs: 5-7 Damian Lundy (b. 1944)

11

Alleluia, alleluia,
give thanks to the risen Lord,
alleluia, alleluia,
give praise to his name.

1. Jesus is Lord of all the earth.
   He is the King of creation.

2. Spread the good news o'er all the earth.
   Jesus has died and is risen.

3. We have been crucified with Christ.
   Now we shall live for ever.

4. God has proclaimed the just reward:
   'Life for us all, alleluia!'

5. Come, let us praise the living God,
   joyfully sing to our Saviour.

Donald Fishel (b. 1950) alt.
© 1973 Word of God Music/CopyCare Ltd

12

1. Amazing grace! How sweet the sound
   that saved a wretch like me.
   I once was lost, but now I'm found;
   was blind but now I see.

2. 'Twas grace that taught my heart to
       fear,
   and grace my fears relieved.
   How precious did that grace appear
   the hour I first believed.

3. Through many dangers, toils and
       snares
   I have already come.
   'Tis grace hath brought me safe thus
       far,
   and grace will lead me home.

4. The Lord has promised good to me,
   his word my hope secures;
   he will my shield and portion be
   as long as life endures.

5. When we've been there a thousand
       years,
   bright shining as the sun,
   we've no less days to sing God's praise
   that when we first begun.

   vs. 1-4: John Newton (1725-1807) alt.,
   vs. 5: John Rees (1828-1900)

13

1. Among us and before us,
   Lord, you stand
   with arms outstretched
   and bread and wine at hand.
   Confronting those
   unworthy of a crumb,
   you ask that to your table
   we should come.

2. Who dare say No,
   when such is your resolve
   our worst to witness,
   suffer and absolve,
   our best to raise in lives
   by God forgiv'n,
   our souls to fill on earth
   with food from heav'n?

3. Who dare say No,
   when such is your intent
   to love the selves
   we famish and resent,
   to cradle our
   uncertainties and fear,
   to kindle hope as
   you in faith draw near?

4. Who dare say No,
   when such is your request
   that each around your table
   should be guest,
   that here the ancient word
   should live as new
   'Take, eat and drink –
   all this is meant for you.'?

5. No more we hesitate
   and wonder why;
   no more we stand indiff'rent,
   scared or shy.
   Your invitation leads us
   to say Yes,
   to meet you where you nourish,
   heal and bless.

   John L. Bell (b. 1949) and Graham Maule (b. 1958)

14

1. An upper room did our Lord prepare
   for those he loved until the end:
   and his disciples still gather there,
   to celebrate their risen friend.

Continued overleaf

2. A lasting gift Jesus gave his own:
to share his bread, his loving cup.
whatever burdens may bow us down,
he by his cross shall lift us up.

3. And after supper he washed their feet
for service, too, is sacrament.
In him our joy shall be made
   complete –
sent out to serve, as he was sent.

4. No end there is! We depart in peace,
he loves beyond our uttermost:
in ev'ry room in our Father's house
he will be there, as Lord and host.

Fred Pratt Green (b. 1903)

15

1. And can it be that I should gain
an in'trest in the Saviour's blood?
Died he for me, who caused his pain?
for me, who him to death pursued?
Amazing love! How can it be
that thou, my God, shouldst die
   for me?

2. 'Tis myst'ry all! th'Immortal dies:
who can explore his strange design?
In vain the first-born seraph tries
to sound the depths of love divine!
'Tis mercy all! Let earth adore,
let angel minds inquire no more.

3. He left his Father's throne above
so free, so infinite his grace;
emptied himself of all but love,
and bled for Adam's helpless race;
'tis mercy all, immense and free;
for, O my God, it found out me.

4. Long my imprisoned spirit lay
fast bound in sin and nature's night;
thine eye diffused a quick'ning ray,
I woke, the dungeon flamed with light;
my chains fell off, my heart was free;
I rose, went forth, and followed thee.

5. No condemnation now I dread;
Jesus, and all in him, is mine!
Alive in him, my living Head,
and clothed in righteousness divine,
bold I approach the eternal throne,
and claim the crown, through Christ
   my own.

Charles Wesley (1707-1788)

16

1. As Jacob with travel
was weary one day,
at night on a stone
for a pillow he lay;
he saw in a vision
a ladder so high
that its foot was on earth
and its top in the sky:

Alleluia to Jesus
who died on the tree,
and has raised up a ladder
of mercy for me,
and has raised up a ladder
of mercy for me.

2. This ladder is long,
it is strong and well-made,
has stood hundreds of years
and is not yet decayed;
many millions have climbed it
and reached Sion's hill,
and thousands by faith
are climbing it still:

3. Come let us ascend!
   all may climb it who will;
   for the angels of Jacob
   are guarding it still:
   and remember, each step
   that by faith we pass o'er,
   some prophet or martyr
   has trod it before:

4. And when we arrive
   at the haven of rest
   we shall hear the glad words,
   'Come up hither, ye blest,
   here are regions of light,
   here are mansions of bliss.'
   O who would not climb
   such a ladder as this?

18th century

17

1. As the deer pants for the water
   so my soul longs after you.
   You alone are my heart's desire
   and I long to worship you.

   You alone are my strength, my shield,
   to you alone may my spirit yield.
   You alone are my heart's desire
   and I long to worship you.

2. I want you more than gold or silver,
   only you can satisfy.
   You alone are the real joy-giver
   and the apple of my eye.

3. You're my friend and you are my
      brother,
   even though you are a king.
   I love you more than any other,
   so much more than anything.

Martin Nystrom, based on Psalm 42:1-2
© 1983 Restoration Music Ltd/
Sovereign Music UK

18

As we are gathered, Jesus is here,
one with each other, Jesus is here,
joined by the Spirit, washed in the blood,
part of the Body, the Church of God.
As we are gathered, Jesus is here,
one with each other, Jesus is here.

John Daniels
© 1979 Springtide/Word Music (UK)/CopyCare Ltd

19

Ascribe greatness to our God, the rock,
his work is perfect and all his ways are
      just.
A God of faithfulness
and without injustice;
good and upright is he.

Peter West, Mary Lou Locke & Mary Kirkbride
© 1979 Peter West/Integrity's Hosanna! Music/
Kingsway's Thankyou Music

20

At this time of giving,
gladly now we bring
gifts of goodness and mercy
from a heav'nly King.

1. Earth could not contain the treasures
   heaven holds for you,
   perfect joy and lasting pleasures,
   love so strong and true.

2. May his tender love surround you
   at this Christmas time;
   may you see his smiling face
   that in the darkness shines.

Continued overleaf

3. But the many gifts he gives
   are all poured out from one;
   come, receive the greatest gift,
   the gift of God's own Son.

   At this time of giving,
   gladly now we bring
   gifts of goodness and mercy
   from a heav'nly King.

   Last two choruses and verses:
   Lai, lai, lai . . . *(Accelerating with each*
   verse)

   Graham Kendrick (b. 1950)
   © 1988 Make Way Music Ltd

21

1. Away in a manger,
   no crib for a bed,
   the little Lord Jesus
   laid down his sweet head.
   The stars in the bright sky
   looked down where he lay,
   the little Lord Jesus,
   asleep on the hay.

2. The cattle are lowing,
   the baby awakes,
   but little Lord Jesus
   no crying he makes.
   I love thee, Lord Jesus!
   Look down from the sky,
   and stay by my side
   until morning is nigh.

3. Be near me, Lord Jesus;
   I ask thee to stay
   close by me for ever,
   and love me, I pray.
   Bless all the dear children
   in thy tender care,
   and fit us for heaven,
   to live with thee there.

An alternative version

1. Away in a manger,
   no crib for a bed,
   the little Lord Jesus
   laid down his sweet head.
   The stars in the bright sky
   looked down where he lay,
   the little Lord Jesus,
   asleep on the hay.

2. The cattle are lowing,
   they also adore
   the little Lord Jesus
   who lies in the straw.
   I love you, Lord Jesus,
   I know you are near
   to love and protect me
   till morning is here.

3. Be near me, Lord Jesus;
   I ask you to stay
   close by me for ever,
   and love me, I pray.
   Bless all the dear children
   in your tender care,
   prepare us for heaven,
   to live with you there.

Original text: William James Kirkpatrick (1838-1921)
Alternative text, vs. 2 & 3: Michael Forster (b. 1946)

22

1. Be still and know that I am God.
   Be still and know that I am God.
   Be still and know that I am God.

2. I am the Lord that healeth thee.
   I am the Lord that healeth thee.
   I am the Lord that healeth thee.

3. In thee, O Lord, I put my trust.
   In thee, O Lord, I put my trust.
   In thee, O Lord, I put my trust.

Unknown, based on Psalm 46

23

1. Be still, for the presence of the Lord,
   the Holy One, is here;
   come, bow before him now,
   with reverence and fear.
   In him no sin is found,
   we stand on holy ground.
   Be still, for the presence of the Lord,
   the Holy One, is here.

2. Be still, for the glory of the Lord
   is shining all around;
   he burns with holy fire,
   with splendour he is crowned.
   How awesome is the sight,
   our radiant King of Light!
   Be still, for the glory of the Lord
   is shining all around.

3. Be still, for the power of the Lord
   is moving in this place,
   he comes to cleanse and heal,
   to minister his grace.
   No work too hard for him,
   in faith receive from him;
   be still, for the power of the Lord
   is moving in this place.

David J. Evans (b. 1957)

© 1986 Kingsway's Thankyou Music

24

1. Be still, my soul:
   the Lord is at your side;
   bear patiently the cross
   of grief and pain;
   leave to your God
   to order and provide;
   in ev'ry change
   he faithful will remain.
   Be still, my soul:
   your best, your heav'nly friend,
   through thorny ways,
   leads to a joyful end.

2. Be still, my soul:
   your God will undertake
   to guide the future
   as he has the past.
   Your hope, your confidence
   let nothing shake,
   all now mysterious
   shall be clear at last.
   Be still, my soul:
   the tempests still obey
   his voice, who ruled them
   once on Galilee.

3. Be still, my soul:
   the hour is hastening on
   when we shall be for ever
   with the Lord,
   when disappointment,
   grief and fear are gone,
   sorrow forgotten,
   love's pure joy restored.
   Be still, my soul:
   when change and tears are past,
   all safe and blessèd
   we shall meet at last.

Katharina Von Schlegal (b. 1697)
trans. Jane L. Borthwick alt.

25

1. Beneath the cross of Jesus
   I fain would take my stand,
   the shadow of a mighty rock
   within a weary land;
   a home within a wilderness,
   a rest upon the way,
   from burning heat at noontide and
   the burden of the day.

2. O safe and happy shelter!
   O refuge tried and sweet!
   O trysting place where heaven's love
   and heaven's justice meet!
   As to the holy patriarch
   that wondrous dream was giv'n,
   so seems my Saviour's cross to me
   a ladder up to heav'n.

3. There lies, beneath its shadow,
   but on the farther side,
   the darkness of an awful grave
   that gapes both deep and wide;
   and there between us stands the cross,
   two arms outstretched to save;
   a watchman set to guard the way
   from that eternal grave.

4. Upon that cross of Jesus
   mine eye at times can see
   the very dying form of One
   who suffered there for me;
   and from my stricken heart, with tears,
   two wonders I confess –
   the wonders of redeeming love,
   and my unworthiness.

5. I take, O cross, thy shadow
   for my abiding place!
   I ask no other sunshine than
   the sunshine of his face;
   content to let the world go by,
   to reckon gain as loss –
   my sinful self, my only shame,
   my glory all – the cross.

Elizabeth C. Clephane (1830-1869) alt.

26

Bind us together, Lord,
bind us together with cords
that cannot be broken.
Bind us together, Lord,
bind us together, Lord,
bind us together in love.

1. There is only one God,
   there is only one King.
   There is only Body,
   that is why we sing:

2. Fit for the glory of God,
   purchased by his precious Blood,
   born with the right to be free:
   Jesus the vict'ry has won.

3. We are the fam'ly of God,
   we are his promise divine,
   we are his chosen desire,
   we are the glorious new wine.

Bob Gillman
© 1977 Kingsway's Thankyou Music

27

Bless the Lord, my soul,
and bless God's holy name.
Bless the Lord, my soul,
who leads me into life.

Taizé Community, from Psalm 103

28

1. Blessed assurance, Jesus is mine:
   O what a foretaste of glory divine!
   Heir of salvation, purchase of God;
   born of his Spirit, washed in his blood

   This is my story, this is my song,
   praising my Saviour all the day long.
   This is my story, this is my song,
   praising my Saviour all the day long.

2. Perfect submission, perfect delight,
   visions of rapture burst on my sight;
   angels descending, bring from above
   echoes of mercy, whispers of love.

3. Perfect submission, all is at rest,
   I in my Saviour am happy and blest;
   watching and waiting, looking above,
   filled with his goodness, lost in his love.

   Frances Jane van Alstyne
   (Fanny J. Crosby) (1820-1915)

29

1. Blest Creator of the light,
   making day with radiance bright,
   thou didst o'er the forming earth
   give the golden light its birth.

2. Thou didst mark the night from day
   with the dawn's first piercing ray;
   darkness now is drawing nigh;
   listen to our humble cry.

3. May we ne'er by guilt depressed
   lose the way to endless rest;
   nor with idle thoughts and vain
   bind our souls to earth again.

4. Rather may we heav'nward rise
   where eternal treasure lies;
   purified by grace within,
   hating ev'ry deed of sin.

5. Holy Father, hear our cry
   through thy Son our Lord most high,
   whom our thankful hearts adore
   with the Spirit evermore.

   'Lucis Creator Optime' trans. unknown

30

1. Born in the night,
   Mary's child,
   a long way from your home;
   coming in need,
   Mary's child,
   born in a borrowed room.

2. Clear shining light,
   Mary's child,
   your face lights up our way;
   light of the world,
   Mary's child,
   dawn on our darkened day.

3. Truth of our life,
   Mary's child,
   you tell us God is good;
   prove it is true,
   Mary's child,
   go to your cross of wood.

4. Hope of the world,
   Mary's child,
   you're coming soon to reign:
   King of the earth,
   Mary's child,
   walk in our streets again.

   Geoffrey Ainger (b. 1925)

31

1. Bread is blessed and broken,
   wine is blessed and poured:
   take this and remember
   Christ the Lord.

2. Share the food of heaven
   earth cannot afford.
   Here is grace in essence –
   Christ the Lord.

3. Know yourself forgiven,
   find yourself restored,
   meet a friend for ever –
   Christ the Lord.

4. God has kept his promise
   sealed by sign and word:
   here, for those who want him –
   Christ the Lord.

John L. Bell (b. 1949) and Graham Maule (b. 1958)
©1978 Sovereign Music UK

32

Broken for me,
broken for you,
the body of Jesus
broken for us.

1. He offered his body,
   he poured out his soul;
   Jesus was broken
   that we might be whole.

2. Come to my table
   and with me dine;
   eat of my bread
   and drink of my wine.

3. This is my body
   given for you;
   eat it, rememb'ring
   I died for you.

4. This is my blood
   I shed for you,
   for your forgiveness,
   making you new.

Janet Lunt
© 1978 Sovereign Music UK

33

1. Brother, sister, let me serve you,
   let me be as Christ to you;
   pray that I may have the grace to
   let you be my servant, too.

2. We are pilgrims on a journey,
   fellow trav'llers on the road;
   we are here to help each other
   walk the mile and bear the load.

3. I will hold the Christlight for you
   in the night-time of your fear;
   I will hold my hand out to you,
   speak the peace you long to hear.

4. I will weep when you are weeping;
   when you laugh I'll laugh with you.
   I will share your joy and sorrow
   till we've seen this journey through.

5. When we sing to God in heaven
   we shall find such harmony,
   born of all we've known together
   of Christ's love and agony.

6. Brother, sister, let me serve you,
   let me be as Christ to you;
   pray that I may have the grace to
   let you be my servant, too.

Richard Gillard
© 1977 Scripture in Song/Integrity's Hosanna! Music

34

By your side I would stay;
in your arms I would lay.
Jesus, lover of my soul,
nothing from you I withhold.
Lord, I love you, and adore you;
what more can I say?
You cause my love to grow stronger
with ev'ry passing day.

Noel and Tricia Richards.
© 1989 Kingsway's Thankyou Music

35

1. Child in the manger, infant of Mary;
   outcast and stranger, Lord of all;
   child who inherits all our
       transgressions,
   all our demerits on him fall.

2. Once the most holy child of salvation
   gently and lowly lived below;
   now as our glorious mighty Redeemer,
   see him victorious o'er each foe.

3. Prophets foretold him, infant of
       wonder;
   angels behold him on his throne;
   worthy our Saviour of all their praises;
   happy for ever are his own.

Mary MacDonald (1817-1890)
trans. Lachlan MacBean (1853-1931)

36

1. Christ is made the sure foundation,
   Christ the head and cornerstone,
   chosen of the Lord, and precious,
   binding all the Church in one,
   holy Sion's help for ever,
   and her confidence alone.

2. To this temple, where we gather,
   come, O Lord of Hosts, today;
   with thy wonted loving-kindness,
   hear thy servants as they pray,
   and thy fullest benediction
   shed within its walls alway.

3. Here vouchsafe to all thy servants
   what they ask of thee to gain,
   what they gain from thee for ever
   with the blessèd to retain,
   and hereafter in thy glory
   evermore with thee to reign.

4. Praise and honour to the Father,
   praise and honour to the Son,
   praise and honour to the Spirit,
   ever Three and ever One,
   consubstantial, co-eternal,
   while unending ages run.

'Urbs beata Jerusalem' (c. 7th century)
trans. John Mason Neale (1818-1866) alt.

37

1. Christ triumphant, ever reigning,
   Saviour, Master, King,
   Lord of heav'n, our lives sustaining,
   hear us as we sing:

   Yours the glory and the crown,
   the high renown, the eternal name.

2. Word incarnate, truth revealing,
   Son of Man on earth!
   Pow'r and majesty concealing
   by your humble birth:

3. Suff'ring servant, scorned, ill-treated,
   victim crucified!
   Death is through the cross defeated,
   sinners justified:

Continued overleaf

4. Priestly King, enthroned for ever
   high in heav'n above!
   Sin and death and hell shall never
   stifle hymns of love:

   Yours the glory and the crown,
   the high renown, the eternal name.

5. So, our hearts and voices raising
   through the ages long,
   ceaselessly upon you gazing,
   this shall be our song:

   Michael Saward (b. 1932)

38

1. Christ's is the world in which we move,
   Christ's are the folk we're summoned
      to love,
   Christ's is the voice which calls us to
      care,
   and Christ is the one who meets us
      here.

   To the lost Christ shows his face;
   to the unloved he gives his embrace;
   to those who cry in pain or disgrace,
   Christ makes with his friends a touching
   place.

2. Feel for the people we most avoid,
   strange or bereaved or never employed;
   feel for the women, and feel for the men
   who fear that their living is all in vain.

3. Feel for the parents who've lost their
      child,
   feel for the women whom men have
      defiled,
   feel for the baby for whom there's no
      breast,
   and feel for the weary who find no rest.

4. Feel for the lives by life confused,
   riddled with doubt, in loving abused;
   feel for the lonely heart, conscious of sin,
   which longs to be pure but fears to
      begin.

   John L. Bell (b. 1949) and Graham Maule (b. 1958)

39

Cloth for the cradle,
cradle for the child,
the child for our ev'ry joy and sorrow;
find him a shawl that's woven by us all
to welcome the Lord
of each tomorrow.

1. Darkness and light
   and all that's known by sight,
   silence and echo fading,
   weave into one a welcome for the Son,
   set earth its own maker serenading.

2. Claimant and queen,
   wage earners in between,
   trader and travelling preacher,
   weave into one a welcome for the Son,
   whose word brings new life to ev'ry
      creature.

3. Hungry and poor,
   the sick and the unsure,
   wealthy, whose needs are stranger,
   weave into one a welcome for the Son,
   leave excess and want beneath the
      manger.

4. Wrinkled or fair,
   carefree or full of care,
   searchers of all the ages,
   weave into one a welcome for the Son,
   the Saviour of shepherds and of sages.

   John L. Bell (b. 1949) and Graham Maule (b. 1958)

40

1. Colours of day dawn into the mind,
   the sun has come up,
   the night is behind.
   Go down in the city, into the street,
   and let's give the message
   to the people we meet.

   So light up the fire
   and let the flame burn,
   open the door, let Jesus return,
   take seeds of his Spirit,
   let the fruit grow,
   tell the people of Jesus,
   let his love show.

2. Go through the park, on into the town;
   the sun still shines on;
   it never goes down.
   The light of the world is risen again;
   the people of darkness
   are needing our friend.

3. Open your eyes, look into the sky,
   the darkness has come,
   the sun came to die.
   The evening draws on,
      the sun disappears,
   but Jesus is living,
   and his Spirit is near.

Sue McClellan (b. 1951), John Paculabo (b.1946)
and Keith Ryecroft (b. 1949)
© 1974 Kingsway's Thankyou Music

41

1. Come and see, come and see,
   come and see the King of love;
   see the purple robe
   and crown of thorns he wears.
   Soldiers mock, rulers sneer
   as he lifts the cruel cross;
   lone and friendless now,
   he climbs towards the hill.

   We worship at your feet,
   where wrath and mercy meet,
   and a guilty world is washed
   by love's pure stream.
   For us he was made sin
   – oh, help me take it in.
   Deep wounds of love cry out 'Father,
   *   forgive'.*
   I worship, I worship the Lamb
   who was slain.

2. Come and weep, come and mourn
   for your sin that pierced him there;
   so much deeper than
   the wounds of thorn and nail.
   All our pride, all our greed,
   all our fallenness and shame;
   and the Lord has laid
   the punishment on him.

3. Man of heav'n, born to earth
   to restore us to your heav'n;
   here we bow in awe
   beneath your searching eyes.
   From your tears comes our joy,
   from your death our life shall spring;
   by your resurrection power
   we shall rise.

Graham Kendrick (b. 1950)
© 1989 Make Way Music Ltd

42

Come, come, come to the manger,
children, come to the children's King;
sing, sing, chorus of angels,
star of morning o'er Bethlehem sing.

1. He lies 'mid the beasts of the stall,
   who is maker and Lord of us all;
   the wintry wind blows cold and dreary,
   see, he weeps, the world is weary;
   Lord, have pity and mercy on me!

2. He leaves all his glory behind,
   to be born and to die for mankind,
   with grateful beasts his cradle chooses,
   thankless world his love refuses;
   Lord, have pity and mercy on me!

3. To the manger of Bethlehem come,
   to the Saviour Emmanuel's home;
   the heav'nly hosts above are singing,
   set the Christmas bells a-ringing;
   Lord, have pity and mercy on me!

   Unknown, alt.

43

1. Come, Holy, Spirit, come!
   inflame our souls with love,
   transforming ev'ry heart and home
   with wisdom from above.
   O let us not despise
   the humble path Christ trod,
   but choose, to shame the worldly wise,
   the foolishness of God.

2. All-knowing Spirit, prove
   the poverty of pride,
   by knowledge of the Father's love
   in Jesus crucified.
   And grant us faith to know
   the glory of that sign,
   and in our very lives to show
   the marks of love divine.

3. Come with the gift to heal
   the wounds of guilt and fear,
   and to oppression's face reveal
   the kingdom drawing near.
   Where chaos longs to reign,
   descend, O holy Dove,
   and free us all to work again
   the miracles of love.

4. Spirit of truth, arise;
   inspire the prophet's voice:
   expose to scorn the tyrant's lies,
   and bid the poor rejoice.
   O Spirit, clear our sight,
   all prejudice remove,
   and help us to discern the right,
   and covet only love.

5. Give us the tongues to speak,
   in ev'ry time and place,
   to rich and poor, to strong and weak,
   the word of love and grace.
   Enable us to hear
   the words that others bring,
   interpreting with open ear
   the special song they sing.

6. Come, Holy Spirit, dance
   within our hearts today,
   our earthbound spirits to entrance,
   our mortal fears allay.
   And teach us to desire,
   all other things above,
   that self-consuming holy fire,
   the perfect gift of love!

   Michael Forster (b.1946) based on 1 Corinthians 12

44

Come on and celebrate!
His gift of love we will celebrate –
the Son of God,
who loved us and gave us life.
We'll shout your praise, O King:
you give us joy nothing else can bring;
we'll give to you our offering
in celebration praise.
Come on and celebrate,
celebrate, celebrate and sing,
celebrate and sing to the King:

Repeat the last three lines.

Patricia Morgan
© 1984 Kingsway's Thankyou Music

45

1. Cry 'Freedom!' in the name of God
   and let the cry resound;
   proclaim for all that freedom
   which in Jesus Christ is found,
   for none of us is truly free
   while anyone is bound.

   Cry 'Freedom!' cry 'Freedom!'
   in God's name, in God's name!
   Cry 'Freedom!' cry 'Freedom!'
   in God's name!

2. Cry 'Freedom!' for the victims
   of the earthquake and the rain:
   where wealthy folk find shelter
   and the poor must bear the pain;
   where weapons claim resources
   while the famine strikes again.

3. Cry 'Freedom!' for dictators
   in their fortresses confined,
   who hide behind their bodyguards
   and fear the open mind,
   and bid them find true freedom
   in the good of humankind.

4. Cry 'Freedom!' in the church when
   honest doubts are met with fear;
   when vacuum-packed theology
   makes questions disappear;
   when journeys end before they start
   and mystery is clear!

5. Cry 'Freedom!' when we find ourselves
   imprisoned in our greed,
   to live in free relationship
   and meet each other's need.
   From self released for others' good
   we should be free indeed!

Michael Forster (b. 1946)

46

Dance and sing, all the earth,
gracious is the hand that tends you:
love and care ev'rywhere,
God on purpose sends you.

1. Shooting star and sunset shape
   the drama of creation;
   lightning flash and moonbeam share
   a common derivation.

2. Deserts stretch and torrents roar
   in contrast and confusion;
   treetops shake and mountains soar
   and nothing is illusion.

3. All that flies and swims and crawls
   displays an animation;
   none can emulate or change
   for each has its own station.

Continued overleaf

4. Brother man and sister woman,
   born of dust and passion,
   praise the one who calls you friends
   and makes you in his fashion.

   Dance and sing, all the earth,
   gracious is the hand that tends you:
   love and care ev'rywhere,
   God on purpose sends you.

5. Kiss of life and touch of death
   suggest our imperfection:
   crib and womb and cross and tomb
   cry out for resurrection.

   John L. Bell (b. 1949) and Graham Maule (b.1958)

47

1. Ding dong! merrily on high,
   in heav'n the bells are ringing;
   ding dong! verily the sky
   is riv'n with angel-singing.
   Gloria, hosanna in excelsis!

2. E'en so here below, below,
   let steeple bells be swungen,
   and io, io, io,
   by priest and people sungen.

3. Pray you, dutifully prime
   your matin chime, ye ringers;
   may you beautifully rhyme
   your evetime song, ye singers.

   George Ratcliffe Woodward (1848-1934)

48

Do not be afraid,
for I have redeemed you.
I have called you by your name;
you are mine.

1. When you walk through the waters,
   I'll be with you.
   You will never sink beneath the waves.

2. When the fire is burning
   all around you,
   you will never be consumed
     by the flames.

3. When the fear of loneliness
   is looming,
   then remember I am at your side.

4. When you dwell in the exile
   of the stranger,
   remember you are precious in my eyes.

5. You are mine, O my child;
   I am your Father,
   and I love you with a perfect love.

   Gerard Markland, based on Isaiah 43:1-4

49

1. Drop, drop, slow tears,
   and bathe those beauteous feet,
   which brought from heav'n
   the news and Prince of peace.

2. Cease not, wet eyes,
   his mercies to entreat;
   to cry for vengeance
   sin doth never cease.

3. In your deep floods
drown all my faults and fears;
nor let his eye
see sin, but through my tears.

Phineas Fletcher (1582-1650)

50

1. Fair waved the golden corn
in Canaan's pleasant land,
when full of joy, some shining morn,
went forth the reaper-band.

2. To God so good and great
their cheerful thanks they pour;
then carry to his temple-gate
the choicest of their store.

3. Like Israel, Lord, we give
our earliest fruits to thee,
and pray that, long as we shall live,
we may thy children be.

4. Thine is our youthful prime,
and life and all its pow'rs;
be with us in our morning time,
and bless our evening hours.

5. In wisdom let us grow,
as years and strength are giv'n,
that we may serve thy Church below,
and join thy saints in heav'n.

John Hampden Gurney (1802-1862)

51

1. Faithful Shepherd, feed me
in the pastures green;
faithful Shepherd, lead me
where thy steps are seen.

2. Hold me fast, and guide me
in the narrow way;
so, with thee beside me,
I shall never stray.

3. Daily bring me nearer
to the heav'nly shore;
may my faith grow clearer,
may I love thee more.

4. Hallow every pleasure,
ev'ry gift and pain;
be thyself my treasure,
though none else I gain.

5. Day by day prepare me
as thou seest best,
then let angels bear me
to thy promised rest.

Thomas Benson Pollock (1836-1896)

52

Father God, I wonder how
I managed to exist
without the knowledge
of your parenthood
and your loving care.
But now I am your child,
I am adopted in your family,
and I can never be alone
'cause, Father God,
you're there beside me.

I will sing your praises,
I will sing your praises,
I will sing your praises
for evermore.

Ian Smale
© 1984 Kingsway's Thankyou Music

53

1. Father, I place into your hands
   the things that I can't do.
   Father, I place into your hands
   the times that I've been through.
   Father, I place into your hands
   the way that I should go,
   for I know I always can trust you.

2. Father, I place into your hands
   my friends and family.
   Father, I place into your hands
   the things that trouble me.
   Father, I place into your hands
   the person I would be,
   for I know I always can trust you.

3. Father, we love to seek your face,
   we love to hear your voice.
   Father, we love to sing your praise,
   and in your name rejoice.
   Father, we love to walk with you
   and in your presence rest,
   for we know we always can trust you.

4. Father, I want to be with you
   and do the things you do.
   Father, I want to speak the words
   that you are speaking too.
   Father, I want to love the ones
   that you will draw to you,
   for I know that I am one with you.

Jenny Hewer (b. 1945)
© 1975 Kingsway's Thankyou Music

54

1. Father, Lord of all creation,
   ground of Being, Life and Love;
   height and depth beyond description
   only life in you can prove:
   you are mortal life's dependence:
   thought, speech, sight are ours by grace;
   yours is ev'ry hour's existence,
   sov'reign Lord of time and space.

2. Jesus Christ, the Man for Others,
   we, your people, make our prayer:
   help us love – as sisters, brothers –
   all whose burdens we can share.
   Where your name binds us together
   you, Lord Christ, will surely be;
   where no selfishness can sever
   there your love the world may see.

3. Holy Spirit, rushing, burning
   wind and flame of Pentecost,
   fire our hearts afresh with yearning
   to regain what we have lost.
   May your love unite our action,
   nevermore to speak alone:
   God, in us abolish faction,
   God, through us your love make known.

Stewart Cross (1928-1989)

55

1. Father, we adore you,
   lay our lives before you.
   How we love you!

2. Jesus, we adore you,
   lay our lives before you.
   How we love you!

3. Spirit, we adore you,
   lay our lives before you.
   How we love you!

Terrye Coelho (b.1952)
© 1972 Maranatha! Music/CopyCare Ltd

56

1. Father, we love you,
   we praise you, we adore you.
   Glorify your name in all the earth.
   Glorify your name, glorify your name,
   glorify your name in all the earth.

2. Jesus, we love you,
   we praise you, we adore you.
   Glorify your name in all the earth.
   Glorify your name, glorify your name,
   glorify your name in all the earth.

3. Spirit, we love you,
   we praise you, we adore you.
   Glorify your name in all the earth.
   Glorify your name, glorify your name,
   glorify your name in all the earth.

Donna Adkins (b. 1940)
© 1976 Maranatha! Music/CopyCare Ltd

57

1. Father, who in Jesus found us,
   God, whose love is all around us,
   who to freedom new unbound us,
   keep our hearts with joy aflame.

2. For the sacramental breaking,
   for the honour of partaking,
   for your life our lives remaking,
   young and old, we praise your name.

3. From the service of this table
   lead us to a life more stable,
   for our witness make us able;
   blessings on our work we claim.

4. Through our calling closely knitted,
   daily to your praise committed,
   for a life of service fitted,
   let us now your love proclaim.

Fred Kaan (b. 1929)

58

1. Fill thou my life, O Lord my God,
   in ev'ry part with praise,
   that my whole being may proclaim
   thy being and thy ways.

2. Not for the lip of praise alone,
   nor e'en the praising heart,
   I ask, but for a life made up
   of praise in ev'ry part.

3. Praise in the common things of life,
   its goings out and in;
   praise in each duty and each deed,
   however small and mean.

4. Fill ev'ry part of me with praise:
   let all my being speak
   of thee and of thy love, O Lord,
   poor though I be and weak.

5. So shalt thou, Lord, receive from me
   the praise and glory due;
   and so shall I begin on earth
   the song for ever new.

6. So shall each fear, each fret, each care,
   be turnèd into song;
   and ev'ry winding of the way
   the echo shall prolong.

7. So shall no part of day or night
   unblest or common be;
   but all my life, in ev'ry step,
   be fellowship with thee.

Horatius Bonar (1808-1889) alt.

59

1. Fill your hearts with joy and gladness,
   sing and praise your God and mine!
   Great the Lord in love and wisdom,
   might and majesty divine!
   He who framed the starry heavens
   knows and names them as they shine.
   Fill your hearts with joy and gladness,
   sing and praise your God and mine!

2. Praise the Lord, his people,
       praise him!
   Wounded souls his comfort know.
   Those who fear him find his mercies,
   peace for pain and joy for woe;
   humble hearts are high exalted,
   human pride and pow'r laid low.
   Praise the Lord, his people,
       praise him!
   Wounded souls his comfort know.

3. Praise the Lord for times and seasons,
   cloud and sunshine, wind and rain;
   spring to melt the snows of winter
   till the waters flow again;
   grass upon the mountain pastures,
   golden valleys thick with grain.
   Praise the Lord for times and seasons,
   cloud and sunshine, wind and rain.

4. Fill your hearts with joy and gladness,
   peace and plenty crown your days!
   Love his laws, declare his judgements,
   walk in all his words and ways;
   he the Lord and we his children,
   praise the Lord, all people, praise!
   Fill your hearts with joy and gladness,
   peace and plenty crown your days!

   Timothy Dudley-Smith (b. 1926)

60

1. Filled with the Spirit's pow'r,
   with one accord
   the infant Church
   confessed its risen Lord.
   O Holy Spirit,
   in the Church today
   no less your pow'r
   of fellowship display.

2. Now with the mind of Christ
   set us on fire,
   that unity
   may be our great desire.
   Give joy and peace;
   give faith to hear your call,
   and readiness
   in each to work for all.

3. Widen our love, good Spirit,
   to embrace
   in your strong care
   the people of each race.
   Like wind and fire
   with life among us move,
   till we are known as Christ's,
   and Christians prove.

   John Raphael Peacey (1896-1971)

61

1. Finished the strife of battle now,
   gloriously crowned the victor's brow;
   sing with gladness, banish sadness:
   Alleluia, alleluia!

2. After the death that him befell,
   Jesus Christ has harrowed hell;
   songs of praising we are raising:
   Alleluia, alleluia!

3. On the third morning he arose,
   shining with vict'ry o'er his foes;
   earth is singing, heav'n is ringing:
   Alleluia, alleluia!

4. Lord, by your wounds on you we call,
   you, by your death, have freed us all;
   may our living be thanksgiving:
   Alleluia, alleluia!

   trans. John Mason Neale (1818-1866) alt.

62

For I'm building a people of power
and I'm making a people of praise,
that will move through this land
by my Spirit,
and will glorify my precious name.
Build your Church, Lord,
make us strong, Lord,
join our hearts, Lord, through your Son.
Make us one, Lord, in your body,
in the kingdom of your Son.

Dave Richards (b. 1947) based on Ephesians 2:21,22
© 1977 Kingsway's Thankyou Music

63

1. For the fruits of his creation,
   thanks be to God;
   for his gifts to ev'ry nation,
   thanks be to God;
   for the ploughing, sowing, reaping,
   silent growth while we are sleeping,
   future needs in earth's safe-keeping,
   thanks be to God.

2. In the just reward of labour,
   God's will is done;
   in the help we give our neighbour,
   God's will is done;
   in our world-wide task of caring
   for the hungry and despairing,
   in the harvests we are sharing,
   God's will is done.

3. For the harvests of his Spirit,
   thanks be to God;
   for the good we all inherit,
   thanks be to God;
   for the wonders that astound us,
   for the truths that still confound us,
   most of all, that love has found us,
   thanks be to God.

   Fred Pratt Green (b. 1903)

64

1. For the healing of the nations,
   Lord, we pray with one accord;
   for a just and equal sharing
   of the things that earth affords.
   To a life of love in action
   help us rise and pledge our word.

2. Lead us, Father, into freedom,
   from despair your world release;
   that, redeemed from war and hatred,
   all may come and go in peace.
   Show us how through care and
      goodness
   fear will die and hope increase.

   Continued overleaf

3. All that kills abundant living,
   let it from the earth be banned;
   pride of status, race or schooling,
   dogmas that obscure your plan.
   In our common quest for justice
   may we hallow life's brief span.

4. You, creator-God, have written
   your great name on humankind;
   for our growing in your likeness,
   bring the life of Christ to mind;
   that by our response and service
   earth its destiny may find.

   Fred Kaan (b. 1929)

65

1. Forty days and forty nights
   in Judah's desert Jesus stayed;
   all alone he fought temptation,
   all alone he fasted, prayed.
   When the heat of passion rules me,
   when I feel alone, betrayed,
   Lord, you meet me in the desert,
   strong in faith and unafraid.

2. In the garden, his disciples
   slept the darkest hours away,
   but our Lord did not condemn them
   when they would not watch or pray.
   Make me constant in your service,
   keeping watch both night and day.
   Give me grace that I may never
   such a love as yours betray.

3. When the rooster crowed at daybreak,
   Peter's fear and panic grew.
   He denied three times the charge
   that Jesus was a man he knew.
   When my love for you is challenged,
   when the faithful ones are few,
   give me courage and conviction
   to proclaim my Lord anew.

4. Soldiers came, the Galilean
   was arrested, bound and tried,
   and upon a wooden cross
   the Son of God was crucified.
   In the darkest hour of torture,
   Jesus raised his head and cried,
   'Why hast thou forsaken me?',
   and faithful to the end, he died.

5. With a sword they pierced his side –
   himself, they jeered, he could not save;
   Joseph then prepared the body
   with sweet spices for the grave.
   This the precious, broken body
   which for me my Saviour gave;
   such a love as his I long for,
   such a faith as his I crave.

   Jean Holloway (b. 1939)

66

1. From heav'n you came, helpless babe,
   entered our world, your glory veiled;
   not to be served but to serve,
   and give your life that we might live.

   This is our God, the Servant King,
   he calls us now to follow him,
   to bring our lives as a daily offering
   of worship to the Servant King.

2. There in the garden of tears,
   my heavy load he chose to bear;
   his heart with sorrow was torn,
   'Yet not my will but yours,' he said.

3. Come see his hands and his feet,
   the scars that speak of sacrifice,
   hands that flung stars into space
   to cruel nails surrendered.

4. So let us learn how to serve,
   and in our lives enthrone him;
   each other's needs to prefer,
   for it is Christ we're serving.

Graham Kendrick (b. 1950)
© *1983 Kingsway's Thankyou Music*

67

1. From many grains,
   once scattered far and wide,
   each one alone, to grow
   as best it may,
   now safely gathered in and unified,
   one single loaf
   we offer here today.
   So may your Church,
   in ev'ry time and place,
   be in this meal
   united by your grace.

2. From many grapes,
   once living on the vine,
   now crushed and broken
   under human feet,
   we offer here this single cup of wine:
   the sign of love,
   unbroken and complete.
   So may we stand
   among the crucified,
   and live the risen life
   of him who died.

3. From many places gathered,
   we are here,
   each with a gift
   that we alone can bring.
   O Spirit of the living God, draw near,
   make whole by grace
   our broken offering.
   O crush the pride
   that bids us stand alone;
   let flow the love
   that makes our spirits one.

Michael Forster (b. 1946)

68

1. From the sun's rising
   unto the sun's setting,
   Jesus our Lord
   shall be great in the earth;
   and all earth's kingdoms
   shall be his dominion,
   all of creation
   shall sing of his worth.

   Let ev'ry heart, ev'ry voice,
   ev'ry tongue join with spirits ablaze;
   one in his love, we will circle the world
   with the song of his praise.
   O let all his people rejoice,
   and let all the earth hear his voice!

2. To ev'ry tongue,
   tribe and nation he sends us,
   to make disciples,
   to teach and baptise;
   for all authority
   to him is given;
   now as his witnesses
   we shall arise.

3. Come let us join
   with the Church from all nations,
   cross ev'ry border,
   throw wide ev'ry door;
   workers with him
   as he gathers his harvest,
   till earth's far corners
   our Saviour adore.

Graham Kendrick (b. 1950)
© *1988 Make Way Music Ltd*

69

1. From the very depths of darkness
   springs a bright and living light,
   out of falsehood and deceit
   a greater truth is brought to sight,
   in the halls of death, defiant,
   life is dancing with delight!
   The Lord is risen indeed!

   Christ is risen! Hallelujah!
   Christ is risen! Hallelujah!
   Christ is risen! Hallelujah!
   The Lord is risen indeed!

2. In the light of resurrection,
   Jesus calls us all by name,
   'Do not cling to what is past,
   for things can never be the same;
   to the trembling and the fearful,
   we've a gospel to proclaim:
   The Lord is risen indeed!'

3. So proclaim it in the high rise,
   in the hostel let it ring,
   make it known in Cardboard City,
   let the homeless rise and sing:
   'He is Lord of life abundant,
   and he changes everything,
   the Lord is risen indeed!'

4. In the heartlands of oppression,
   sound the cry of liberty,
   where the poor are crucified,
   behold the Lord of Calvary!
   From the fear of death and dying,
   Christ has set his people free!
   The Lord is risen indeed!

5. Tell the despots and dictators
   of a love that can't be known
   in a guarded palace-tomb,
   condemned to live and die alone:
   'Take the risk of love and freedom;
   Christ has rolled away the stone!
   The Lord is risen indeed!'

6. When our spirits are entombed
   in mortal prejudice and pride,
   when the gates of hell itself
   are firmly bolted from inside,
   at the bidding of his Spirit,
   we may fling them open wide!
   The Lord is risen indeed!

   Michael Forster (b. 1946)

70

Gather around, for the table is spread,
welcome the food and rest!
Wide is our circle, with Christ at the
    head,
he is the honoured guest.
Learn of his love, grow in his grace,
pray for the peace he gives;
here at this meal, here in this place,
know that his spirit lives!
Once he was known
in the breaking of bread,
shared with a chosen few;
multitudes gathered
and by him were fed,
so will he feed us too.

Jean Holloway (b. 1939)

71

1. Give me joy in my heart,
   keep me praising,
   give me joy in my heart, I pray.
   Give me joy in my heart,
   keep me praising,
   keep me praising till the end of day.

Sing hosanna! Sing hosanna!
Sing hosanna to the King of kings!
Sing hosanna! Sing hosanna!
Sing hosanna to the King!

2. Give me peace in my heart,
   keep me resting,
   give me peace in my heart, I pray.
   Give me peace in my heart,
   keep me resting,
   keep me resting till the end of day.

3. Give me love in my heart,
   keep me serving,
   give me love in my heart, I pray.
   Give me love in my heart,
   keep me serving,
   keep me serving till the end of day.

4. Give me oil in my lamp,
   keep me burning,
   give me oil in my lamp, I pray.
   Give me oil in my lamp,
   keep me burning,
   keep me burning till the end of day.

Traditional

72

Give thanks with a grateful heart,
give thanks to the Holy One;
give thanks because he's given
Jesus Christ, his Son.
Give thanks with a grateful heart,
give thanks to the Holy One;
give thanks because he's given
Jesus Christ, his Son.
And now let the weak say 'I am strong',
let the poor say 'I am rich',
because of what the Lord has done for us;
and now let the weak say 'I am strong',
let the poor say 'I am rich',
because of what the Lord has done for us.

Henry Smith
© 1978 Integrity's Hosanna! Music/
Kingsway's Thankyou Music

73

1. Give to our God immortal praise;
   mercy and truth are all his ways:
   wonders of grace to God belong,
   repeat his mercies in your song.

2. Give to the Lord of lords renown,
   the King of kings with glory crown:
   his mercies ever shall endure
   when earthly pow'rs are known no
      more.

3. He sent his Son with pow'r to save
   from guilt and darkness and the grave:
   wonders of grace to God belong,
   repeat his mercies in your song.

4. Through earthly life he guides our feet,
   and leads us to his heav'nly seat:
   his mercies ever shall endure
   when earthly pow'rs are known no
      more.

Isaac Watts (1674-1748) based on Psalm 136 alt.

74

Gloria, gloria in excelsis Deo!
Gloria, gloria, alleluia, alleluia!

From Scripture

75

1. Glory to God, glory to God,
   glory to the Father.
   Glory to God, glory to God,
   glory to the Father.
   To him be glory for ever.
   To him be glory for ever.
   Alleluia, amen.
   Alleluia, amen,
   alleluia, amen,
   alleluia, amen.

2. Glory to God, glory to God,
   Son of the Father.
   Glory to God, glory to God,
   Son of the Father.
   To him be glory for ever.
   To him be glory for ever.
   Alleluia, amen.
   Alleluia, amen,
   alleluia, amen,
   alleluia, amen.

3. Glory to God, glory to God,
   glory to the Spirit.
   Glory to God, glory to God,
   glory to the Spirit.
   To him be glory for ever.
   To him be glory for ever.
   Alleluia, amen.
   Alleluia, amen,
   alleluia, amen,
   alleluia, amen.

Traditional Peruvian,
collected by John Ballantine (b. 1945)

76

1. Glory to thee, O God,
   for all thy saints in light,
   who nobly strove and conquered
   in the well fought fight.
   Their praises sing,
   who life outpoured
   by fire and sword for Christ their King.

2. Thanks be to thee, O Lord,
   for saints thy Spirit stirred
   in humble paths to live thy life and
   speak thy word.
   Unnumbered they,
   whose candles shine
   to lead our footsteps after thine.

3. Lord God of truth and love,
   'thy kingdom come', we pray;
   give us thy grace to know thy truth and
   walk thy way:
   that here on earth
   thy will be done,
   till saints in earth and heav'n are one.

Howard Charles Adie Gaunt (1902-1983)

77

1. Go forth and tell!
   O Church of God, awake!
   God's saving news
   to all the nations take:
   proclaim Christ Jesus,
   Saviour, Lord and King,
   that all the world
   his worthy praise may sing.

2. Go forth and tell!
   God's love embraces all;
   he will in grace
   respond to all who call;
   how shall they call
   if they have never heard
   the gracious invitation
   of his word?

3. Go forth and tell!
   where still the darkness lies;
   in wealth or want,
   the sinner surely dies:
   give us, O Lord,
   concern of heart and mind,
   a love like yours
   which cares for humankind.

4. Go forth and tell!
   the doors are open wide:
   share God's good gifts –
   let no-one be denied;
   live out your life
   as Christ your Lord shall choose,
   your ransomed pow'rs
   for his sole glory use.

5. Go forth and tell!
   O Church of God, arise!
   Go in the strength
   which Christ your Lord supplies;
   go till all nations
   his great name adore
   and serve him, Lord and King,
   for evermore.

   James Edward Seddon (1915-1983)

78

Go, tell it on the mountain,
over the hills and ev'rywhere.
Go, tell it on the mountain
that Jesus Christ is born.

1. While shepherds kept their watching
   o'er wand'ring flocks by night,
   behold, from out of heaven,
   there shone a holy light.

2. And lo, when they had seen it,
   they all bowed down and prayed;
   they travelled on together
   to where the babe was laid.

3. When I was a seeker,
   I sought both night and day:
   I asked my Lord to help me
   and he showed me the way.

4. He made me a watchman
   upon the city wall,
   and, if I am a Christian,
   I am the least of all.

   Traditional

79

1. God forgave my sin in Jesus' name.
   I've been born again in Jesus' name.
   And in Jesus' name I come to you
   to share his love as he told me to.

He said: 'Freely, freely
you have received;
freely, freely give.
Go in my name,
and because you believe,
others will know that I live.'

Continued overleaf

2. All pow'r is giv'n in Jesus' name,
   in earth and heav'n in Jesus' name.
   And in Jesus' name I come to you
   to share his pow'r as he told me to.

   He said: 'Freely, freely
   you have received;
   freely, freely give.
   Go in my name,
   and because you believe,
   others will know that I live.'

3. God gives us life in Jesus' name,
   he lives in us in Jesus' name.
   And in Jesus' name I come to you
   to share his peace as he told me to.

Carol Owens
© *1972 Bud John Songs/Alliance Media Ltd/CopyCare Ltd*

80

God is good, we sing and shout it,
God is good, we celebrate.
God is good, no more we doubt it,
God is good, we know it's true.
(*Last Time* Hey!)

And when I think of his love for me,
my heart fills with praise
and I feel like dancing.
For in his heart there is room for me
and I run with arms opened wide.

Graham Kendrick (b. 1950)
© *1985 Kingsway's Thankyou Music*

81

1. God is love: his the care,
   tending each, ev'rywhere.
   God is love, all is there!
   Jesus came to show him,
   that mankind might know him!

Sing aloud, loud, loud!
Sing aloud, loud, loud!
God is good! God is truth!
God is beauty! Praise him!

2. None can see God above;
   we can share life and love;
   thus may we Godward move,
   seek him in creation,
   holding ev'ry nation.

3. Jesus lived on the earth,
   life and hope brought to birth
   and affirmed human worth,
   for he came to save us
   by the truth he gave us.

4. To our Lord praise we sing,
   light and life, friend and king,
   coming down, love to bring,
   pattern for our duty,
   showing God in beauty.

Percy Dearmer (1867-1936) alt.

82

1. God is our strength from days of old,
   the hope of ev'ry nation;
   whose pow'r conceived the universe
   and set the earth's foundation.
   Though hidden from our sight
   in uncreated light,
   his presence yet is known,
   his wondrous purpose shown
   resplendent in creation!

2. That Word of Life, before all things
   in primal darkness spoken,
   became for us the Word made flesh
   for our redemption broken.
   His glory set aside,
   for us he lived and died,
   obedient to the death,
   renewed in life and breath,
   to endless glory woken!

3. That Breath of God, who brooded first
   upon the new creation,
   who lit with light the Virgin's womb
   to bear the world's salvation;
   that Dove whose shadow graced
   th'anointed Saviour's face,
   now challenges us all
   to recognise the call
   to hope and liberation.

4. O great Creator, Spirit, Word,
   the well-spring of creation,
   our Alpha and our Omega,
   our hope and our salvation;
   to Father, Spirit, Son,
   the Three for ever One,
   and One for ever Three,
   mysterious Trinity,
   be praise and adoration.

Michael Forster (b. 1946)

83

1. God is working his purpose out
   as year succeeds to year.
   God is working his purpose out,
   and the day is drawing near.
   Nearer and nearer draws the time,
   the time that shall surely be,
   when the earth shall be filled
   with the glory of God
   as the waters cover the sea.

2. From the east to the utmost west
   wherever foot has trod,
   through the mouths of his messengers
   echoes forth the voice of God:
   'Listen to me, ye continents,
   ye islands, give ear to me,
   that the earth shall be filled
   with the glory of God
   as the waters cover the sea.'

3. How can we do the work of God,
   how prosper and increase
   harmony in the human race
   and the reign of perfect peace?
   What can we do to urge the time,
   the time that shall surely be,
   when the earth shall be filled
   with the glory of God
   as the waters cover the sea?

4. March we forth in the strength of God,
   his banner is unfurled;
   let the light of the gospel shine
   in the darkness of the world:
   strengthen the weary, heal the sick
   and set ev'ry captive free,
   that the earth shall be filled
   with the glory of God
   as the waters cover the sea.

5. All our efforts are nothing worth
   unless God bless the deed;
   vain our hopes for the harvest tide
   till he brings to life the seed.
   Yet ever nearer draws the time,
   the time that shall surely be,
   when the earth shall be filled
   with the glory of God
   as the waters cover the sea.

Arthur Campbell Ainger (1841-1919)
adapted by Michael Forster (b. 1946)

84

1. God moves in a mysterious way
   his wonders to perform;
   he plants his footsteps in the sea,
   and rides upon the storm.

2. Deep in unfathomable mines
   of never-failing skill,
   he treasures up his bright designs,
   and works his sov'reign will.

3. Ye fearful saints, fresh courage take;
   the clouds ye so much dread
   are big with mercy, and shall break
   in blessings on your head.

4. Judge not the Lord by feeble sense,
   but trust him for his grace;
   behind a frowning providence
   he hides a shining face.

5. His purposes will ripen fast,
   unfolding ev'ry hour;
   the bud may have a bitter taste,
   but sweet will be the flow'r.

6. Blind unbelief is sure to err,
   and scan his work in vain;
   God is his own interpreter,
   and he will make it plain.

   William Cowper (1731-1800)

85

1. God of grace and God of glory,
   on thy people pour thy pow'r;
   now fulfil thy Church's story;
   bring her bud to glorious flow'r.
   Grant us wisdom, grant us courage,
   for the facing of this hour.

2. Lo, the hosts of evil round us
   scorn thy Christ, assail his ways;
   from the fears that long have bound us
   free our hearts to faith and praise.
   Grant us wisdom, grant us courage,
   for the living of these days.

3. Cure thy children's warring madness,
   bend our pride to thy control;
   shame our wanton selfish gladness,
   rich in goods and poor in soul.
   Grant us wisdom, grant us courage,
   lest we miss thy kingdom's goal.

4. Set our feet on lofty places,
   gird our lives that they may be
   armoured with all Christlike graces
   as we set your people free.
   Grant us wisdom, grant us courage,
   lest we fail the world or thee.

   Harry Emerson Fosdick (1878-1969) alt.

86

1. God rest you merry, gentlemen,
   let nothing you dismay,
   for Jesus Christ our Saviour
   was born on Christmas day,
   to save us all from Satan's pow'r
   when we were gone astray:

   O tidings of comfort and joy,
   comfort and joy,
   O tidings of comfort and joy.

2. In Bethlehem, in Jewry,
   this blessèd babe was born,
   and laid within a manger,
   upon this blessèd morn;
   the which his mother Mary
   did nothing take in scorn.

3. From God, our heav'nly Father,
   a blessèd angel came,
   and unto certain shepherds
   brought tidings of the same,
   how that in Bethlehem was born
   the Son of God by name.

4. 'Fear not,' then said the angel,
   'let nothing you affright,
   this day is born a Saviour,
   of virtue, pow'r and might;
   by him the world is overcome
   and Satan put to flight.'

5. The shepherds at those tidings
   rejoicèd much in mind,
   and left their flocks a-feeding,
   in tempest, storm and wind,
   and went to Bethlehem straightway
   this blessèd babe to find.

6. But when to Bethlehem they came,
   whereat this infant lay,
   they found him in a manger,
   where oxen feed on hay;
   his mother Mary kneeling,
   unto the Lord did pray.

7. Now to the Lord sing praises,
   all you within this place,
   and with true love and fellowship
   each other now embrace;
   this holy tide of Christmas
   all others doth deface.

Traditional English alt.

87

1. God, whose farm is all creation,
   take the gratitude we give;
   take the finest of our harvest,
   crops we grow that all may live.

2. Take our ploughing, seeding, reaping,
   hopes and fears of sun and rain,
   all our thinking, planning, waiting,
   ripened in this fruit and grain.

3. All our labour, all our watching,
   all our calendar of care,
   in these crops of your creation,
   take, O God: they are our prayer.

John Arlott (1914-1991) alt.

88

1. Good Christians all, rejoice
   with heart and soul and voice!
   Give ye heed to what we say:
   News! News!
   Jesus Christ is born today;
   ox and ass before him bow,
   and he is in the manger now:
   Christ is born today,
   Christ is born today!

2. Good Christians all, rejoice
   with heart and soul and voice!
   Now ye hear of endless bliss:
   Joy! Joy!
   Jesus Christ was born for this.
   He hath opened heaven's door,
   and we are blest for evermore:
   Christ was born for this,
   Christ was born for this.

3. Good Christians all, rejoice
   with heart and soul and voice!
   Now ye need not fear the grave:
   Peace! Peace!
   Jesus Christ was born to save;
   calls you one, and calls you all,
   to gain his everlasting hall:
   Christ was born to save,
   Christ was born to save.

John Mason Neale (1818-1866) alt.

89

1. Good King Wenceslas looked out
   on the feast of Stephen,
   when the snow lay round about,
   deep, and crisp, and even:
   brightly shone the moon that night,
   though the frost was cruel,
   when a poor man came in sight,
   gath'ring winter fuel.

2. 'Hither, page, and stand by me,
   if thou know'st it, telling,
   yonder peasant, who is he,
   where and what his dwelling?'
   'Sire, he lives a good league hence,
   underneath the mountain,
   right against the forest fence,
   by Saint Agnes' fountain.'

3. 'Bring me flesh, and bring me wine,
   bring me pine logs hither:
   thou and I will see him dine,
   when we bring them thither.'
   Page and monarch, forth they went,
   forth they went together;
   through the rude wind's wild lament,
   and the bitter weather.

4. 'Sire, the night is darker now,
   and the wind blows stronger;
   fails my heart, I know not how;
   I can go no longer.'
   'Mark my footsteps good, my page;
   tread thou in them boldly:
   thou shalt find the winter's rage
   freeze thy blood less coldly.'

5. In his master's steps he trod,
   where the snow lay dinted;
   heat was in the very sod
   which the Saint had printed.
   Therefore, Christians all, be sure,
   wealth or rank possessing,
   ye who now will bless the poor,
   shall yourselves find blessing.

John Mason Neale (1818-1866) alt.

90

Great is the Lord
and most worthy of praise,
the city of our God, the holy place,
the joy of the whole earth.
Great is the Lord
in whom we have the victory,
he aids us against the enemy,
we bow down on our knees.
And, Lord,
we want to lift your name on high,
and, Lord, we want to thank you
for the works you've done in our lives,
and, Lord,
we trust in your unfailing love,
for you alone are God eternal,
throughout earth and heaven above.

Steve McEwan
©1985 Body Songs/CopyCare Ltd

91

1. Great is thy faithfulness,
   O God my Father,
   there is no shadow
   of turning with thee;
   thou changest not,
   thy compassions, they fail not;
   as thou hast been
   thou for ever wilt be.

Great is thy faithfulness!
Great is thy faithfulness!
Morning by morning
new mercies I see;
all I have needed
thy hand hath provided,
great is thy faithfulness,
Lord, unto me!

2. Summer and winter,
   and springtime and harvest,
   sun, moon and stars
   in their courses above,
   join with all nature
   in manifold witness
   to thy great faithfulness,
   mercy and love.

3. Pardon for sin
   and a peace that endureth,
   thine own dear presence
   to cheer and to guide;
   strength for today
   and bright hope for tomorrow,
   blessings all mine,
   with ten thousand beside!

Thomas Obadiah Chisholm (1866-1960)
© 1951 Hope Publishing Co.

92

1. Great Son of God,
   you once on Cal'vry's cross
   fought the long fight
   for truth and freedom's sake,
   endured the scourge,
   the crown of thorns,
   the nails that fixed
   your youthful body to a stake.
   For six long hours
   you suffered searing pain
   to set your captive
   people free again.

2. 'Give us a sign from heav'n,'
   the people cried.
   'If you are Christ,
   leap down, alive and free.
   Who could accept as Saviour
   one who died
   like some poor miscreant
   skewered to a tree?'
   Lord Christ, our Saviour,
   you would not descend
   until your glorious work
   achieved its end.

3. 'My God, my God,
   where have you gone?' you called,
   alone and helpless,
   willing still to share
   through all the gath'ring
   gloom of Calvary,
   the depth of dying sinners'
   deep despair.
   But then triumphant,
   ready now to die,
   'The work is finished!'
   was your glorious cry.

Edwin Le Grice (1911-1992)

93

1. Hail, gladdening Light,
   of his pure glory poured
   from the immortal Father,
   heav'nly, blest,
   holiest of holies,
   Jesus Christ our Lord.

2. Now we are come
   to the sun's hour of rest,
   the lights of evening
   round us shine,
   we hymn the Father,
   Son and Holy Spirit divine.

Continued overleaf

3. Worthiest art thou at all times
   to be sung with undefilèd tongue,
   Son of our God,
   giver of life, alone:
   therefore in all the world thy glories,
   Lord, they own.

Greek (3rd century or earlier)
trans. John Keble (1792-1866)

4. Worship, honour, pow'r and blessing,
   thou art worthy to receive;
   loudest praises, without ceasing,
   it is right for us to give:
   help, ye bright angelic spirits!
   bring your sweetest, noblest lays;
   help to sing our Saviour's merits,
   help to chant Immanuel's praise.

John Bakewell (1721-1819) alt.

94

1. Hail, thou once despisèd Jesus,
   hail, thou Galilean King!
   Thou didst suffer to release us;
   thou didst free salvation bring.
   Hail, thou universal Saviour,
   bearer of our sin and shame;
   by thy merits we find favour;
   life is given through thy name.

2. Paschal Lamb, by God appointed,
   all our sins on thee were laid;
   by almighty love anointed,
   thou hast full atonement made.
   All thy people are forgiven
   through the virtue of thy blood;
   opened is the gate of heaven,
   we are reconciled to God.

3. Jesus, hail! enthroned in glory,
   there for ever to abide;
   all the heav'nly hosts adore thee,
   seated at thy Father's side:
   there for sinners thou art pleading,
   there thou dost our place prepare;
   ever for us interceding,
   till in glory we appear.

95

Hallelujah, my Father,
for giving us your Son;
sending him into the world
to be given up for all,
knowing we would bruise him
and smite him from the earth!
Hallelujah, my Father,
in his death is my birth.
Hallelujah, my Father,
in his life is my life.

Tim Cullen, alt.
© 1975 Celebration/Kingsway's Thankyou Music

96

1. Hark, my soul, it is the Lord;
   'tis thy Saviour, hear his word;
   Jesus speaks, and speaks to thee,
   'Say, poor sinner, lov'st thou me?

2. 'I delivered thee when bound,
   and, when wounded, healed thy wound;
   sought thee wand'ring, set thee right,
   turned thy darkness into light.

3. 'Can a woman's tender care
cease towards the child she bare?
yes, she may forgetful be,
yet will I remember thee.

4. 'Mine is an unchanging love,
higher than the heights above,
deeper than the depths beneath,
free and faithful, strong as death.

5. 'Thou shalt see my glory soon,
when the work of grace is done;
partner of my throne shalt be:
say, poor sinner, lov'st thou me?'

6. Lord, it is my chief complaint
that my love is weak and faint;
yet I love thee, and adore;
O for grace to love thee more!

William Cowper (1731-1800) based on John 21:16

97

1. Have faith in God, my heart,
trust and be unafraid;
God will fulfil in ev'ry part
each promise he has made.

2. Have faith in God, my mind,
though oft thy light burns low;
God's mercy holds a wiser plan
than thou canst fully know.

3. Have faith in God, my soul,
his Cross for ever stands;
and neither life nor death can pluck
his children from his hands.

4. Lord Jesus, make me whole;
grant me no resting-place,
until I rest, heart, mind and soul,
the captive of thy grace.

Bryn Austin Rees (1911-1983)

98

1. Have you heard the raindrops
drumming on the rooftops?
Have you heard the raindrops
dripping on the ground?
Have you heard the raindrops
splashing in the streams
and running to the rivers all around?

There's water, water of life
Jesus gives us the water of life;
there's water, water of life,
Jesus gives us the water of life.

2. There's a busy worker
digging in the desert,
digging with a spade
that flashes in the sun;
soon there will be water
rising in the well-shaft,
spilling from the bucket as it comes.

3. Nobody can live
who hasn't any water,
when the land is dry
then nothing much grows;
Jesus gives us life
if we drink the living water,
sing it so that ev'rybody knows.

Christian Strover

99

He is exalted,
the King is exalted on high;
I will praise him.
He is exalted,
for ever exalted
and I will praise his name!
He is the Lord;
for ever his truth shall reign.
Heaven and earth rejoice
in his holy name.
He is exalted,
the King is exalted on high.

Twila Paris
© 1985 Straightway Music/Alliance Media Ltd/CopyCare Ltd

100

1. He is Lord, he is Lord.
   He is risen from the dead
   and he is Lord.
   Ev'ry knee shall bow,
   ev'ry tongue confess
   that Jesus Christ is Lord.

2. He is King, he is King.
   He is risen from the dead
   and he is King.
   Ev'ry knee shall bow,
   ev'ry tongue confess
   that Jesus Christ is King.

3. He is love, he is love.
   He is risen from the dead
   and he is love.
   Ev'ry knee shall bow,
   ev'ry tongue confess
   that Jesus Christ is love.

Unknown

101

1. He's got the whole world in his hand.
   He's got the whole world in his hand.
   He's got the whole world in his hand.
   He's got the whole world in his hand.

2. He's got you and me, brother, in his
   hand. (3)
   He's got the whole world in his hand.

3. He's got you and me, sister, in his
   hand. (3)
   He's got the whole world in his hand.

4. He's got the little tiny baby in his
   hand. (3)
   He's got the whole world in his hand.

5. He's got ev'rybody here in his hand. (3)
   He's got the whole world in his hand.

Traditional

102

1. Heav'n shall not wait
   for the poor to lose their patience,
   the scorned to smile,
   the despised to find a friend:
   Jesus is Lord,
   he has championed the unwanted;
   in him injustice
   confronts its timely end.

2. Heav'n shall not wait
   for the rich to share their fortunes,
   the proud to fall,
   the élite to tend the least:
   Jesus is Lord;
   he has shown the masters' privilege –
   to kneel and wash
   servants' feet before they feast.

3. Heav'n shall not wait
for the dawn of great ideas,
thoughts of compassion
divorced from cries of pain:
Jesus is Lord;
he has married word and action;
his cross and company
make his purpose plain.

4. Heav'n shall not wait
for our legalised obedience,
defined by statute,
to strict conventions bound:
Jesus is Lord;
he has hallmarked true allegiance –
goodness appears
where his grace is sought and found.

5. Heav'n shall not wait
for triumphant hallelujahs,
when earth has passed
and we reach another shore:
Jesus is Lord
in our present imperfection;
his pow'r and love
are for now and then for evermore.

John L. Bell (b. 1949) and Graham Maule (b. 1958)

103

1. Help us to help each other, Lord,
each other's cross to bear;
let each a helping hand afford,
and feel each other's care.

2. Up into thee, our living head,
let us in all things grow,
and by thy sacrifice be led
the fruits of love to show.

3. Drawn by the magnet of thy love
let all our hearts agree;
and ever t'wards each other move,
and ever move t'wards thee.

4. This is the bond of perfectness,
thy spotless charity.
O let us still we pray, possess
the mind that was in thee.

After Charles Wesley (1707-1788) alt.

104

1. Holy, holy, holy, holy.
Holy, holy, holy Lord
God almighty;
and we lift our hearts before you
as a token of our love,
holy, holy, holy, holy.

2. Gracious Father, gracious Father,
we are glad to be your children,
gracious Father;
and we lift our heads before you
as a token of our love,
gracious Father, gracious Father.

3. Risen Jesus, risen Jesus,
we are glad you have redeemed us,
risen Jesus;
and we lift our hands before you
as a token of our love,
risen Jesus, risen Jesus.

4. Holy Spirit, Holy Spirit,
come and fill our hearts anew,
Holy Spirit;
and we lift our voice before you
as a token of our love,
Holy Spirit, Holy Spirit.

5. Hallelujah, hallelujah,
hallelujah, hallelujah,
hallelujah;
and we lift our hearts before you
as a token of our love,
hallelujah, hallelujah.

Jimmy Owens
© Bud John Songs/Alliance Media Ltd/Copycare Ltd

105

1. Holy, holy, holy is the Lord,
   holy is the Lord God almighty.
   Holy, holy, holy is the Lord,
   holy is the Lord God almighty:
   who was, and is, and is to come;
   holy, holy, holy is the Lord.

2. Jesus, Jesus, Jesus is the Lord,
   Jesus is the Lord God almighty:
   Jesus, Jesus, Jesus is the Lord,
   Jesus is the Lord God almighty:
   who was, and is, and is to come;
   Jesus, Jesus, Jesus is the Lord.

3. Worthy, worthy, worthy is the Lord,
   worthy is the Lord God almighty:
   worthy, worthy, worthy is the Lord,
   worthy is the Lord God almighty:
   who was, and is, and is to come;
   worthy, worthy, worthy is the Lord.

4. Glory, glory, glory to the Lord,
   glory to the Lord God almighty:
   glory, glory, glory to the Lord,
   glory to the Lord God almighty:
   who was, and is, and is to come;
   glory, glory, glory to the Lord.

Unknown

106

1. Hosanna, hosanna,
   hosanna in the highest!
   Hosanna, hosanna,
   hosanna in the highest!
   Lord, we lift up your name
   with hearts full of praise;
   be exalted, O Lord, our God!
   Hosanna in the highest!

2. Glory, glory,
   glory to the King of kings!
   Glory, glory,
   glory to the King of kings!
   Lord, we lift up your name
   with hearts full of praise;
   be exalted, O Lord, our God!
   Glory to the King of kings!

Carl Tuttle, based on Matthew 21:9
© 1985 Mercy/Vineyard Publishing/Integrity's Hosanna! Music

107

1. How firm a foundation,
   ye saints of the Lord,
   is laid for your faith
   in his excellent word;
   what more can he say
   than to you he hath said,
   you who unto Jesus
   for refuge have fled?

2. Fear not, he is with thee,
   O be not dismayed;
   for he is thy God,
   and will still give thee aid:
   he'll strengthen thee, help thee,
   and cause thee to stand,
   upheld by his righteous,
   omnipotent hand.

3. In ev'ry condition,
   in sickness, in health,
   in poverty's vale,
   or abounding in wealth;
   at home and abroad,
   on the land, on the sea,
   as thy days may demand
   shall thy strength ever be.

4. When through the deep waters
   he calls thee to go,
   the rivers of grief
   shall not thee overflow;
   for he will be with thee
   in trouble to bless,
   and sanctify to thee
   thy deepest distress.

5. When through fiery trials
   thy pathway shall lie,
   his grace all-sufficient
   shall be thy supply;
   the flame shall not hurt thee,
   his only design
   thy dross to consume
   and thy gold to refine.

6. The soul that on Jesus
   has leaned for repose
   he will not, he cannot,
   desert to its foes;
   that soul, though all hell
   should endeavour to shake,
   he never will leave,
   he will never forsake.

   Richard Keen (c. 1787)

108

1. How good is the God we adore!
   Our faithful, unchangeable friend:
   his love is as great as his pow'r
   and knows neither measure nor end.

2. For Christ is the first and the last;
   his Spirit will guide us safe home;
   we'll praise him for all that is past
   and trust him for all that's to come.

   Joseph Hart (1712-1768)

109

1. How lovely on the mountains
   are the feet of him
   who brings good news, good news,
   announcing peace,
   proclaiming news of happiness:
   our God reigns, our God reigns.

2. You watchmen, lift your voices
   joyfully as one,
   shout for your King, your King!
   See eye to eye,
   the Lord restoring Sion:
   our God reigns, our God reigns.

3. Waste places of Jerusalem,
   break forth with joy!
   We are redeemed, redeemed.
   The Lord has saved
   and comforted his people:
   our God reigns, our God reigns.

4. Ends of the earth,
   see the salvation of our God!
   Jesus is Lord, is Lord!
   Before the nations,
   he has bared his holy arm:
   our God reigns, our God reigns.

   Based on Isaiah 52, v.1: Leonard E. Smith Jnr.
   (b. 1942) vs. 2-4: unknown
   © 1974 Kingsway's Thankyou Music

110

I am a new creation,
no more in condemnation,
here in the grace of God I stand.
My heart is overflowing,
my love just keeps on growing,
here in the grace of God I stand.
And I will praise you, Lord,
yes, I will praise you, Lord,
and I will sing of all that you have done.
A joy that knows no limit,
a lightness in my spirit,
here in the grace of God I stand.

Dave Bilbrough
© 1983 Kingsway's Thankyou Music

111

1. I am the bread of life.
   You who come to me shall not hunger;
   and who believe in me shall not thirst.
   No-one can come to me
   unless the Father beckons.

   And I will raise you up,
   and I will raise you up,
   and I will raise you up on the last day.

2. The bread that I will give
   is my flesh for the life of the world,
   and if you eat of this bread,
   you shall live for ever,
   you shall live for ever.

3. Unless you eat
   of the flesh of the Son of Man,
   and drink of his blood,
   and drink of his blood,
   you shall not have life within you.

4. I am the resurrection,
   I am the life.
   If you believe in me,
   even though you die,
   you shall live for ever.

5. Yes, Lord, I believe
   that you are the Christ,
   the Son of God,
   who has come
   into the world.

Suzanne Toolan (b. 1927)

112

1. I am trusting thee, Lord Jesus,
   trusting only thee;
   trusting thee for full salvation,
   great and free.

2. I am trusting thee for pardon,
   at thy feet I bow;
   for thy grace and tender mercy,
   trusting now.

3. I am trusting thee for cleansing
   in the crimson flood;
   trusting thee to make me holy
   by thy blood.

4. I am trusting thee to guide me;
   thou alone shalt lead,
   ev'ry day and hour supplying
   all my need.

5. I am trusting thee for power,
   thine can never fail;
   words which thou thyself shalt give me
   must prevail.

6. I am trusting thee, Lord Jesus;
   never let me fall;
   I am trusting thee for ever,
   and for all.

Frances Ridley Havergal (1836-1879)

113

1. I believe in Jesus;
   I believe he is the Son of God.
   I believe he died and rose again.
   I believe he paid for us all.
   And I believe he's here now
   standing in our midst;
   here with the power to heal now,
   and the grace to forgive.

2. I believe in you, Lord;
   I believe you are the Son of God.
   I believe you died and rose again.
   I believe you paid for us all.
   And I believe you're here now
   standing in our midst;
   here with the power to heal now,
   and the grace to forgive.

Marc Nelson
© 1987 Mercy/Vineyard Publishing/Integrity's Hosanna! Music

114

1. I bind unto myself today
   the strong name of the Trinity,
   by invocation of the same,
   Three in One and One in Three.

2. I bind this day to me for ever,
   by pow'r of faith, Christ's incarnation,
   his baptism in the Jordan river,
   his death on cross for my salvation;
   his bursting from the spicèd tomb,
   his riding up the heav'nly way,
   his coming at the day of doom,
   I bind unto myself today.

3. I bind unto myself the pow'r
   of the great love of cherubim;
   the sweet 'Well done!' in judgement
      hour;
   the service of the seraphim,
   confessors' faith, apostles' word,
   the patriarchs' prayers, the prophets'
      scrolls,
   all good deeds done unto the Lord,
   and purity of faithful souls.

PART TWO

4. Christ be with me, Christ within me,
   Christ behind me, Christ before me.
   Christ beside me, Christ to win me,
   Christ to comfort and restore me.
   Christ beneath me, Christ above me,
   Christ in quiet, Christ in danger,
   Christ in hearts of all that love me,
   Christ in mouth of friend and stranger.

DOXOLOGY

5. I bind unto myself the name,
   the strong name of the Trinity,
   by invocation of the same,
   the Three in One and One in Three,
   of whom all nature hath creation,
   eternal Father, Spirit, Word.
   Praise to the Lord of my salvation:
   salvation is of Christ the Lord.
   Amen.

ascribed to St. Patrick (373-463),
trans. Cecil Frances Alexander (1818-1895) alt.

115

1. I cannot tell
how he whom angels worship
should stoop to love
the peoples of the earth,
or why as shepherd
he should seek the wand'rer
with his mysterious promise
of new birth.
But this I know,
that he was born of Mary,
when Bethl'em's manger
was his only home,
and that he lived at
Nazareth and laboured,
and so the Saviour,
Saviour of the world, is come.

2. I cannot tell
how silently he suffered,
as with his peace
he graced this place of tears,
or how his heart
upon the cross was broken,
the crown of pain
to three and thirty years.
But this I know,
he heals the broken-hearted,
and stays our sin,
and calms our lurking fear,
and lifts the burden
from the heavy laden,
for yet the Saviour,
Saviour of the world, is here.

3. I cannot tell
how he will win the nations,
how he will claim
his earthly heritage,
how satisfy
the needs and aspirations
of east and west,
of sinner and of sage.
But this I know,
all flesh shall see his glory,
and he shall reap
the harvest he has sown,
and some glad day
his sun shall shine in splendour
when he the Saviour,
Saviour of the world, is known.

4. I cannot tell
how all the lands shall worship,
when, at his bidding,
ev'ry storm is stilled,
or who can say
how great the jubilation
when ev'ry heart
with perfect love is filled.
But this I know,
the skies will thrill with rapture,
and myriad, myriad
human voices sing,
and earth to heav'n,
and heav'n to earth, will answer:
'At last the Saviour,
Saviour of the world, is King!'

William Young Fullerton (1857-1932) alt.

116

1. I come with joy, a child of God,
forgiven, loved and free,
the life of Jesus to recall,
in love laid down for me.

2. I come with Christians far and near
   to find, as all are fed,
   the new community of love
   in Christ's communion bread.

3. As Christ breaks bread, and bids us
       share,
   each proud division ends.
   The love that made us, makes us one,
   and strangers now are friends.

4. The Spirit of the risen Christ,
   unseen, but ever near,
   is in such friendship better known,
   alive among us here.

5. Together met, together bound
   by all that God has done,
   we'll go with joy, to give the world
   the love that makes us one.

   Brian A. Wren (b. 1936)

117

1. 'I do not know the man,'
   the fearful Peter said.
   No sharper nail could pierce the hand
   by which the world is fed,
   by which the world is fed!

2. The great disciple failed;
   his weakness we may own,
   and stand with him where judgement
       meets
   with grace, at Calv'ry's throne,
   with grace, at Calv'ry's throne.

3. Christ stands among us still,
   in those the world denies,
   and in the faces of the poor,
   we see his grieving eyes,
   we see his grieving eyes.

4. We cannot cleanse our hands
   of that most shameful spot,
   since of our brother we have said,
   'His keeper, I am not!'
   'His keeper, I am not!'

5. And yet, what love is this?
   Forgiveness all divine!
   Christ says of our poor faithless souls,
   'I know them, they are mine.'
   'I know them, they are mine.'

   Michael Forster (b. 1946)

118

1. I give you all the honour
   and praise that's due your name,
   for you are the King of Glory,
   the Creator of all things.

   And I worship you,
   I give my life to you,
   I fall down on my knees.
   Yes, I worship you,
   I give my life to you,
   I fall down on my knees.

2. As your Spirit moves upon me now,
   you meet my deepest need,
   and I lift my hands up to your throne,
   your mercy I've received.

3. You have broken chains that bound
       me,
   you've set this captive free;
   I will lift my voice to praise your name
   for all eternity.

   Carl Tuttle
   © *1982 Mercy/Vineyard Publishing/Integrity's Hosanna! Music*

119

1. I know that my Redeemer lives!
   What joy the blest assurance gives!
   He lives, he lives, who once was dead;
   he lives, my everlasting Head!

2. He lives, to bless me with his love;
   he lives, to plead for me above;
   he lives, my hungry soul to feed;
   he lives, to help in time of need.

3. He lives, and grants me daily breath;
   he lives – for me he conquered death;
   he lives, my mansion to prepare;
   he lives, to lead me safely there.

4. He lives, all glory to his name;
   he lives, my Saviour, still the same;
   what joy the blest assurance gives!
   I know that my Redeemer lives!

   Samuel Medley (1738-1799) alt.

120

I love you, Lord,
and I lift my voice to worship you;
O my soul, rejoice.
Take joy, my King, in what you hear,
may it be a sweet, sweet sound
in your ear.

Laurie Klein
© *1978 Marantha! Music/CopyCare Ltd*

121

1. I need thee ev'ry hour,
   most gracious Lord;
   no tender voice like thine
   can peace afford.

I need thee, O I need thee!
ev'ry hour I need thee;
O bless me now,
my Saviour! I come to thee.

2. I need thee ev'ry hour;
   stay thou near by;
   temptations lose their pow'r
   when thou art nigh.

3. I need thee ev'ry hour,
   in joy or pain;
   come quickly and abide,
   or life is vain.

4. I need thee ev'ry hour;
   teach me thy will,
   and thy rich promises
   in me fulfil.

5. I need thee ev'ry hour,
   most Holy One;
   O make me thine indeed,
   thou blessèd Son!

   Annie Sherwood Hawks (1835-1918)

122

1. I, the Lord of sea and sky,
   I have heard my people cry.
   All who dwell in dark and sin
   my hand will save.
   I who made the stars of night,
   I will make their darkness bright.
   Who will bear my light to them?
   Whom shall I send?

Here I am, Lord. Is it I, Lord?
I have heard you calling in the night.
I will go, Lord, if you lead me.
I will hold your people in my heart.

2. I, the Lord of snow and rain,
   I have borne my people's pain.
   I have wept for love of them.
   They turn away.
   I will break their hearts of stone,
   give them hearts for love alone.
   I will speak my word to them.
   Whom shall I send?

3. I, the Lord of wind and flame,
   I will tend the poor and lame.
   I will set a feast for them.
   My hand will save.
   Finest bread I will provide
   till their hearts be satisfied.
   I will give my life to them.
   Whom shall I send?

Dan Schutte, based on Isaiah 6
© 1981 Daniel L. Schutte & New Dawn Music

123

I will enter his gates
with thanksgiving in my heart,
I will enter his courts with praise.
I will say this is the day
that the Lord has made.
I will rejoice
for he has made me glad.
He has made me glad.
He has made me glad.
I will rejoice
for he has made me glad.
He has made me glad.
He has made me glad.
I will rejoice
for he has made me glad.

Leona von Brethorst, based on Scripture
© 1976 Maranatha! Music/CopyCare Ltd

124

1. I will sing the wondrous story
   of the Christ who died for me,
   how he left the realms of glory
   for the cross on Calvary.
   Yes, I'll sing the wondrous story
   of the Christ who died for me –
   sing it with his saints in glory,
   gathered by the crystal sea.

2. I was lost but Jesus found me,
   found the sheep that went astray,
   raised me up and gently led me
   back into the narrow way.
   Days of darkness still may meet me,
   sorrow's path I oft may tread;
   but his presence still is with me,
   by his guiding hand I'm led.

3. He will keep me till the river
   rolls its waters at my feet:
   then he'll bear me safely over,
   made by grace for glory meet.
   Yes, I'll sing the wondrous story
   of the Christ who died for me –
   sing it with his saints in glory,
   gathered by the crystal sea.

Francis Harold Rawley (1854-1952)
© HarperCollins Religious/CopyCare Ltd

125

1. I wonder as I wander
   out under the sky,
   how Jesus the Saviour
   did come for to die
   for poor ord'n'ry people
   like you and like I.
   I wonder as I wander
   out under the sky.

Continued overleaf

2. When Mary birthed Jesus,
   'twas in a cow's stall
   with wise men and farmers
   and shepherds and all.
   But high from God's heaven
   a star's light did fall,
   and the promise of ages
   it did then recall.

3. If Jesus had wanted
   for any wee thing,
   a star in the sky,
   or a bird on the wing,
   or all of God's angels
   in heav'n for to sing,
   he surely could have it,
   'cause he was the King.

Traditional North American

126

I'm accepted, I'm forgiven,
I am fathered by the true
and living God.
I'm accepted, no condemnation,
I am loved by the true
and living God.
There's no guilt or fear as I draw near
to the Saviour
and Creator of the world.
There is joy and peace as I release
my worship to you, O Lord.

Rob Hayward
© 1985 Kingsway's Thankyou Music

127

1. I'm not ashamed to own my Lord,
   or to defend his cause;
   maintain the honour of his word,
   the glory of his cross.

2. Jesus, my God, I know his name;
   his name is all my trust;
   nor will he put my soul to shame,
   nor let my hope be lost.

3. Firm as his throne his promise stands;
   and he can well secure
   what I've committed to his hands,
   till the decisive hour.

4. Then will he own my worthless name
   before his Father's face;
   and in the new Jerusalem
   appoint my soul a place.

Isaac Watts (1674-1748)

128

1. If I were a butterfly,
   I'd thank you, Lord,
   for giving me wings,
   and if I were a robin in a tree,
   I'd thank you, Lord, that I could sing,
   and if I were a fish in the sea,
   I'd wiggle my tail
   and I'd giggle with glee,
   but I just thank you,
   Father, for making me me.

   For you gave me a heart
   and you gave me a smile,
   you gave me Jesus
   and you made me your child,
   and I just thank you,
   Father, for making me me.

2. If I were an elephant,
   I'd thank you, Lord,
   by raising my trunk,
   and if I were a kangaroo,
   you know I'd hop right up to you,
   and if I were an octopus,
   I'd thank you, Lord,
   for my fine looks,
   but I just thank you, Father,
   for making me me.

3. If I were a wiggly worm,
   I'd thank you, Lord,
   that I could squirm,
   and if I were a billy goat,
   I'd thank you, Lord,
      for my strong throat,
   and if I were a fuzzy wuzzy bear,
   I'd thank you, Lord,
   for my fuzzy wuzzy hair,
   but I just thank you, Father,
   for making me me.

Brian Howard
© 1974 Celebration/Kingsway's Thankyou Music

129

1. In full and glad surrender,
   I give myself to thee,
   thine utterly and only
   and evermore to be.

2. O Son of God, who lov'st me,
   I will be thine alone;
   and all I have and am, Lord,
   shall henceforth be thine own!

3. Reign over me, Lord Jesus,
   O make my heart thy throne;
   it shall be thine, dear Saviour,
   it shall be thine alone.

4. O come and reign, Lord Jesus,
   rule over ev'rything!
   And keep me always loyal
   and true to thee, my King.

Frances Ridley Havergal (1836-1879)

130

1. In heav'nly love abiding,
   no change my heart shall fear;
   and safe is such confiding,
   for nothing changes here.
   The storm may roar without me,
   my heart may low be laid,
   but God is round about me,
   and can I be dismayed?

2. Wherever he may guide me,
   no want shall turn me back;
   my Shepherd is beside me,
   and nothing can I lack.
   His wisdom ever waketh,
   his sight is never dim,
   he knows the way he taketh,
   and I will walk with him.

3. Green pastures are before me,
   which yet I have not seen;
   bright skies will soon be o'er me,
   where the dark clouds have been.
   My hope I cannot measure,
   my path to life is free,
   my Saviour has my treasure,
   and he will walk with me.

Anna Laetitia Waring (1820-1910) based on Psalm 23

131

1. In the Cross of Christ I glory,
   tow'ring o'er the wrecks of time;
   all the light of sacred story
   gathers round its head sublime.

2. When the woes of life o'ertake me,
   hopes deceive, and fears annoy,
   never shall the Cross forsake me;
   Lo! it glows with peace and joy.

3. When the sun of bliss is beaming
   light and love upon my way,
   from the Cross the radiance streaming
   adds more lustre to the day.

4. Bane and blessing, pain and pleasure,
   by the Cross are sanctified;
   peace is there that knows no measure,
   joys that through all time abide.

   John Bowring (1792-1872) based on Galatians 6:14

132

In the Lord I'll be ever thankful,
in the Lord I will rejoice!
Look to God, do not be afraid;
lift up your voices: the Lord is near,
lift up your voices: the Lord is near.

Taizé Community

133

1. Infant holy, infant lowly,
   for his bed a cattle stall;
   oxen lowing, little knowing
   Christ the babe is Lord of all.
   Swift are winging angels singing,
   nowells ringing, tidings bringing,
   Christ the babe is Lord of all,
   Christ the babe is Lord of all.

2. Flocks were sleeping, shepherds keeping
   vigil till the morning new;
   saw the glory, heard the story,
   tidings of a gospel true.
   Thus rejoicing, free from sorrow,
   praises voicing, greet the morrow,
   Christ the babe was born for you,
   Christ the babe was born for you.

   From the Polish
   trans. Edith Margaret Gellibrand Reed (1885-1933)

134

1. Inspired by love and anger,
   disturbed by endless pain,
   aware of God's own bias,
   we ask him once again:
   'How long must some folk suffer?
   How long can few folk mind?
   How long dare vain self-int'rest
   turn prayer and pity blind?'

2. From those for ever victims
   of heartless human greed,
   their cruel plight composes
   a litany of need:
   'Where are the fruits of justice?
   Where are the signs of peace?
   When is the day when pris'ners
   and dreams find their release?'

3. From those for ever shackled
   to what their wealth can buy,
   the fear of lost advantage
   provokes the bitter cry:
   'Don't query our position!
   Don't criticise our wealth!
   Don't mention those exploited
   by politics and stealth!'

4. To God, who through the prophets
   proclaimed a diff'rent age,
   we offer earth's indiff'rence,
   its agony and rage:
   'When will the wronged be righted?
   When will the kingdom come?
   When will the world be gen'rous
   to all instead of some?'

5. God asks: 'Who will go for me?
   Who will extend my reach?
   And who, when few will listen,
   will prophesy and preach?
   And who, when few bid welcome,
   will offer all they know?
   And who, when few dare follow,
   will walk the road I show?'

6. Amused in someone's kitchen,
   asleep in someone's boat,
   attuned to what the ancients
   exposed, proclaimed and wrote,
   a Saviour without safety,
   a tradesman without tools
   has come to tip the balance
   with fishermen and fools.

   John L. Bell (b. 1949) and Graham Maule (b. 1958)

135

1. It fell upon a summer day,
   when Jesus walked in Galilee,
   the mothers from a village
   brought their children to his knee.

2. He took them in his arms, and laid
   his hands on each remembered head;
   'Allow these little ones to come
   to me,' he gently said.

3. 'Forbid them not: unless ye bear
   the childlike heart your hearts within,
   unto my kingdom ye may come,
   but may not enter in.'

4. My Lord, I fain would enter there;
   O let me follow thee, and share
   thy meek and lowly heart, and be
   freed from all worldly care.

5. O happy thus to live and move,
   and sweet this world, where I shall find
   God's beauty everywhere, his love,
   his good in humankind.

6. Then, Father, grant this childlike heart,
   that I may come to Christ, and feel
   his hands on me in blessing laid,
   love-giving, strong to heal.

   Stopford Augustus Brooke (1832-1916) alt.

136

It's me, it's me, it's me, O Lord,
standing in the need of prayer.
It's me, it's me, it's me, O Lord,
standing in the need of prayer.

1. Not my brother or my sister,
   but it's me, O Lord,
   standing in the need of prayer.
   Not my brother or my sister,
   but it's me, O Lord,
   standing in the need of prayer.

2. Not my mother or my father,
   but it's me, O Lord,
   standing in the need of prayer.
   Not my mother or my father,
   but it's me, O Lord,
   standing in the need of prayer.

Continued overleaf

3. Not the stranger or my neighbour,
   but it's me, O Lord,
   standing in the need of prayer.
   Not the stranger or my neighbour,
   but it's me, O Lord,
   standing in the need of prayer.

   It's me, it's me, it's me, O Lord,
   standing in the need of prayer.
   It's me, it's me, it's me, O Lord,
   standing in the need of prayer.

   Spiritual

137

1. 'James and Andrew, Peter and John,
   men of temper, talent and tide,
   your nets are empty, empty and bare.
   Cast them now on the opposite side.'

2. 'Jesus, you're only a carpenter's son:
   joints and joists are part of your trade,
   but ours the skill to harvest the deep.
   Why presume to come to our aid?'

3. 'Friends of mine and brothers through
   love,
   I mean more than fishing for food.
   I call your skill to service my will,
   call your lives to harvest the good.'

4. 'Cast your nets where you think is
   right;
   spend your lives where you think is
   need;
   but if you long for that which is best,
   let it be on my word you feed.'

5. 'Stir then the waters, Lord, stir up the
   wind;
   stir the hope that needs to be stretched;
   stir up the love that needs to be
   ground;
   stir the faith that needs to be fetched.'

6. James and Andrew, Peter and John,
   and the women close by his side,
   hear how the Lord calls each by their
   name,
   asking all to turn like the tide.

   John L. Bell (b. 1949) and Graham Maule (b. 1958)

138

1. Jerusalem, my happy home,
   name ever dear to me,
   when shall my labours have an end?
   thy joys when shall I see?

2. Apostles, martyrs, prophets, there
   around my Saviour stand;
   and all I love in Christ below
   will join the glorious band.

3. Jerusalem, my happy home,
   when shall I come to thee?
   when shall my labours have an end?
   thy joys when shall I see?

4. O Christ, do thou my soul prepare
   for that bright home of love;
   that I may see thee and adore
   with all thy saints above.

   Based on verses by F. B. P.,
   an unknown author (c. 1600)

139

1. Jesus Christ is waiting,
   waiting in the streets;
   no-one is his neighbour,
   all alone he eats.
   Listen, Lord Jesus,
   I am lonely too;
   make me, friend or stranger,
   fit to wait on you.

2. Jesus Christ is raging,
   raging in the streets
   where injustice spirals
   and all hope retreats.
   Listen, Lord Jesus,
   I am angry too;
   in the kingdom's causes
   let me rage with you.

3. Jesus Christ is healing,
   healing in the streets;
   curing those who suffer,
   touching those he greets.
   Listen, Lord Jesus,
   I have pity too;
   let my care be active,
   healing just like you.

4. Jesus Christ is dancing,
   dancing in the streets,
   where each sign of hatred
   his strong love defeats.
   Listen, Lord Jesus,
   I feel triumph too;
   on suspicion's graveyard,
   let me dance with you.

5. Jesus Christ is calling,
   calling in the streets,
   'Come and walk faith's tightrope,
   I will guide your feet.'
   Listen, Lord Jesus,
   let my fears be few;
   walk one step before me,
   I will follow you.

John L. Bell (b. 1949) and Graham Maule (b. 1958)

140

1. Jesus is Lord!
   Creation's voice proclaims it,
   for by his pow'r each tree and flow'r
   was planned and made.
   Jesus is Lord!
   The universe declares it;
   sun, moon and stars in heaven cry:
   Jesus is Lord!

Jesus is Lord!
Jesus is Lord!
Praise him with hallelujahs,
for Jesus is Lord.

2. Jesus is Lord!
   Yet from his throne eternal
   in flesh he came to die in pain
   on Calv'ry's tree.
   Jesus is Lord!
   From him all life proceeding,
   yet gave his life a ransom
   thus setting us free.

3. Jesus is Lord!
   O'er sin the mighty conqu'ror,
   from death he rose and all his foes
   shall own his name.
   Jesus is Lord!
   God sends his Holy Spirit
   to show by works of power
   that Jesus is Lord.

David J. Mansell

141

Jesus, Jesus,
holy and anointed one, Jesus.
Jesus, Jesus,
risen and exalted one, Jesus.
Your name is like honey on my lips,
your Spirit like water to my soul.
Your word is a lamp unto my feet.
Jesus, I love you, I love you.
Jesus, Jesus,
holy and anointed one, Jesus.
Jesus, Jesus,
risen and exalted one, Jesus.

John Barnett
© 1988 Mercy/Vineyard Publishing/Integrity's Hosanna! Music

142

Jesus, name above all names,
beautiful Saviour, glorious Lord,
Emmanuel, God with us,
blessèd Redeemer, living Word.

Naida Hearn (b. 1944)
© 1974 Scripture in Song/Integrity's Hosanna! Music

143

1. Jesus, Prince and Saviour,
   Lord of life who died;
   Christ, the friend of sinners,
   mocked and crucified;
   for a world's salvation,
   he his body gave,
   lay at last death's victim,
   lifeless in the grave.

   Lord of life triumphant,
   risen now to reign!
   King of endless ages,
   Jesus lives again!

2. In his pow'r and Godhead
   ev'ry vict'ry won;
   pain and passion ended,
   all his purpose done.
   Christ the Lord is risen!
   sighs and sorrows past,
   death's dark night is over,
   morning comes at last!

3. Resurrection morning!
   sinners' bondage freed;
   Christ the Lord is risen –
   he is ris'n indeed!
   Jesus, Prince and Saviour,
   Lord of Life who died,
   Christ the King of Glory
   now is glorified!

Timothy Dudley-Smith (b. 1926)

144

1. Jesus put this song into our hearts,
   Jesus put this song into our hearts;
   it's a song of joy
   no-one can take away.
   Jesus put this song into our hearts.

2. Jesus taught us how to live in harmony,
   Jesus taught us how to live in harmony;
   diff'rent faces, diff'rent races,
   he made us one.
   Jesus taught us how to live in harmony.

3. Jesus taught us how to be a family,
   Jesus taught us how to be a family,
   loving one another
   with the love that he gives.
   Jesus taught us how to be a family.

4. Jesus turned our sorrow into dancing,
Jesus turned our sorrow into dancing;
changed our tears of sadness
into rivers of joy.
Jesus turned our sorrow into a dance.

Each verse should be sung faster

145

Jesus, remember me
when you come into your kingdom.
Jesus, remember me
when you come into your kingdom.

Based on Scripture

146

Jesus shall take the highest honour,
Jesus shall take the highest praise;
let all earth join heav'n in exalting
the name which is
above all other names.
Let's bow the knee
in humble adoration,
for at his name ev'ry knee must bow;
let ev'ry tongue confess he is Christ,
God's only Son.
Sov'reign Lord, we give you glory now,
for all honour and blessing
and power belongs to you,
belongs to you.
All honour and blessing
and power belongs to you,
belongs to you,
Lord Jesus Christ,
Son of the living God.

147

1. Jesus, stand among us
at the meeting of our lives,
be our sweet agreement
at the meeting of our eyes.

*O Jesus, we love you,
so we gather here,
join our hearts in unity
and take away our fear.*

2. So to you we're gath'ring
out of each and ev'ry land,
Christ the love between us
at the joining of our hands.

Optional verse for Communion

3. Jesus stand among us
at the breaking of the bread;
join us as one body
as we worship you, our Head.

148

*Jesus took a piece of bread,
he shared a cup of wine.
'Eat and drink with me,' he said,
'because you're friends of mine!'*

1. We eat and drink with Jesus
because we are his friends,
remembering his promise
of life that never ends.

2. We share with one another
the bread and wine he gives,
and celebrate together
the special life he lives.

Continued overleaf

3. We rise up from the table,
   and go where Jesus sends,
   to tell the world the gospel
   of love that never ends.

   Jesus took a piece of bread,
   he shared a cup of wine.
   'Eat and drink with me,' he said,
   'because you're friends of mine!'

   Michael Forster (b. 1946)

150

Jubilate, ev'rybody,
serve the Lord in all your ways,
and come before his presence singing;
enter now his courts with praise.
For the Lord our God is gracious,
and his mercy everlasting.
Jubilate, jubilate, jubilate Deo!

Fred Dunn (1907-1979)
© 1977 Kingsway's Thankyou Music

149

1. Joy to the world! The Lord is come;
   let earth receive her King;
   let ev'ry heart prepare him room
   and heav'n and nature sing,
   and heav'n and nature sing,
   and heav'n, and heav'n and nature sing!

2. Joy to the earth! The Saviour reigns;
   let us our songs employ;
   while fields and floods, rocks, hills and
       plains
   repeat the sounding joy,
   repeat the sounding joy,
   repeat, repeat the sounding joy.

3. He rules the world with truth and grace,
   and makes the nations prove
   the glories of his righteousness,
   and wonders of his love,
   and wonders of his love,
   and wonders, and wonders of his love.

   Isaac Watts (1674-1748) alt.

151

1. Judge eternal, throned in splendour,
   Lord of lords and King of kings,
   with thy living fire of judgement
   purge this realm of bitter things:
   solace all its wide dominion
   with the healing of thy wings.

2. Still the weary folk are pining
   for the hour that brings release:
   and the city's crowded clangour
   cries aloud for sin to cease;
   and the homesteads and the
       woodlands
   plead in silence for their peace.

3. Crown, O God, thine own endeavour;
   cleave our darkness with thy sword;
   feed thy people's hungry spirits
   with the richness of thy word:
   cleanse the body of this nation
   through the glory of the Lord.

   Henry Scott Holland (1847-1918) alt.

152

1. Just a closer walk with thee,
   grant it, Jesus, if you please;
   daily walking close to thee,
   let it be, dear Lord, let it be.

2. Through the day of toil that's near,
   if I fall, dear Lord, who cares?
   Who with me my burden shares?
   None but thee, dear Lord, none but
      thee.

3. When my feeble life is o'er,
   time for me will be no more.
   Guide me gently, safely on
   to the shore, dear Lord, to the shore.

Traditional

153

1. Kum ba yah, my Lord, kum ba yah,
   kum ba yah, my Lord, kum ba yah,
   kum ba yah, my Lord, kum ba yah,
   O Lord, kum ba yah.

2. Someone's crying, Lord, kum ba yah,
   someone's crying, Lord, kum ba yah,
   someone's crying, Lord, kum ba yah,
   O Lord, kum ba yah.

3. Someone's singing, Lord, kum ba yah,
   someone's singing, Lord, kum ba yah,
   someone's singing, Lord, kum ba yah,
   O Lord, kum ba yah.

4. Someone's praying, Lord, kum ba yah,
   someone's praying, Lord, kum ba yah,
   someone's praying, Lord, kum ba yah,
   O Lord, kum ba yah.

Spiritual

154

Kyrie, Kyrie, eleison.

From the Roman Missal

155

Latin text

Laudate Dominum,
laudate Dominum,
omnes gentes, alleluia!
Laudate Dominum,
laudate Dominum,
omnes gentes, alleluia!

English text

Sing, praise and bless the Lord.
Sing, praise and bless the Lord,
peoples! nations! Alleluia!
Sing, praise and bless the Lord.
Sing, praise and bless the Lord,
peoples! nations! Alleluia!

Taizé Community (Psalm 117)

156

1. Led like a lamb to the slaughter,
   in silence and shame,
   there on your back you carried a world
   of violence and pain.
   Bleeding, dying, bleeding, dying.

   *You're alive, you're alive,
   you have risen!
   Alleluia! And the pow'r
   and the glory is given,
   alleluia! Jesus to you.*

Continued overleaf

2. At break of dawn, poor Mary,
   still weeping she came,
   when through her grief she heard your
      voice
   now speaking her name.
   Mary, Master, Mary, Master.

   You're alive, you're alive,
   you have risen!
   Alleluia! And the pow'r
   and the glory is given,
   alleluia! Jesus to you.

3. At the right hand of the Father
   now seated on high
   you have begun your eternal reign
   of justice and joy.
   Glory, glory, glory, glory.

   Graham Kendrick (b. 1950)
   © 1983 Kingsway's Thankyou Music

157

1. Let there be love shared among us,
   let there be love in our eyes.
   May now your love sweep this nation;
   cause us, O Lord, to arise.
   Give us a fresh understanding,
   brotherly love that is real.
   Let there be love shared among us,
   Let there be love.

2. Let there be peace shared among us,
   let there be peace in our eyes.
   May now your peace sweep this nation;
   cause us, O Lord, to arise.
   Give us a fresh understanding,
   sisterly love that is real.
   Let there be peace shared among us,
   let there be peace.

3. Let there be hope shared among us,
   let there be hope in our eyes.
   May now your hope sweep this nation;
   cause us, O Lord, to arise.
   Give us a fresh understanding,
   brotherly love that is real.
   Let there be hope shared among us,
   let there be hope.

4. Let there be joy shared among us,
   let there be joy in our eyes.
   May now your joy sweep this nation;
   cause us, O Lord, to arise.
   Give us a fresh understanding,
   sisterly love that is real.
   Let there be joy shared among us,
   let there be joy.

5. Let there be love shared among us,
   let there be love in our eyes.
   May now your love sweep this nation;
   cause us, O Lord, to arise.
   Give us a fresh understanding,
   brotherly love that is real.
   Let there be love shared among us,
   let there be love.

   Dave Bilbrough
   © 1979 Kingway's Thankyou Music

158

1. Let us break bread together
   on our knees,
   let us break bread together
   on our knees.
   When I fall on my knees
   with my face to the rising sun,
   O Lord, have mercy on me.

2. Let us share wine together
   on our knees,
   let us share wine together
   on our knees.
   When I fall on my knees
   with my face to the rising sun,
   O Lord, have mercy on me.

3. Let us praise God together
   on our knees,
   let us praise God together
   on our knees.
   When I fall on my knees
   with my face to the rising sun,
   O Lord, have mercy on me.

Unknown

159

1. Let us praise God together, let us
   praise;
   let us praise God together all our days.
   He is faithful in all his ways,
   he is worthy of all our praise,
   his name be exalted on high.

2. Let us seek God together, let us pray;
   let us seek his forgiveness as we pray.
   He will cleanse us from all sin,
   he will help us the fight to win,
   his name be exalted on high.

3. Let us serve God together, him obey;
   let our lives show his goodness
   through each day.
   Christ the Lord is the world's true
   light,
   let us serve him with all our might,
   his name be exalted on high.

James Edward Seddon (1915-1983)

160

1. Let us talents and tongues employ,
   reaching out with a shout of joy:
   bread is broken, the wine is poured,
   Christ is spoken and seen and heard.

   Jesus lives again,
   earth can breathe again,
   pass the word around:
   loaves abound!

2. Christ is able to make us one,
   at his table he sets the tone,
   teaching people to live to bless,
   love in word and in deed express.

3. Jesus calls us in, sends us out
   bearing fruit in a world of doubt,
   gives us love to tell, bread to share:
   God-Immanuel everywhere!

Fred Kaan (b. 1929)

161

Lift high the Cross,
the love of Christ proclaim
till all the world
adore his sacred name!

1. Come, Christians, follow
   where our Saviour trod,
   o'er death victorious,
   Christ the Son of God.

2. Led on their way
   by this triumphant sign,
   the hosts of God
   in joyful praise combine:

Continued overleaf

3. Each new disciple
   of the Crucified
   is called to bear
   the seal of him who died:

   Lift high the Cross,
   the love of Christ proclaim
   till all the world
   adore his sacred name!

4. Saved by the Cross
   whereon their Lord was slain,
   now Adam's children
   their lost home regain:

5. From north and south,
   from east and west they raise
   in growing harmony
   their song of praise:

6. O Lord, once lifted
   on the glorious tree,
   as thou hast promised,
   draw us unto thee:

7. Let ev'ry race
   and ev'ry language tell
   of him who saves
   from fear of death and hell:

8. From farthest regions,
   let them homage bring,
   and on his Cross
   adore their Saviour King:

9. Set up thy throne,
   that earth's despair may cease
   beneath the shadow
   of its healing peace:

10. For thy blest Cross
    which doth for all atone,
    creation's praises
    rise before thy throne:

11. So let the world
    proclaim with one accord
    the praises of
    our everliving Lord.

George William Kitchin (1827-1912)
and Michael Robert Newbolt (1874-1956) alt.

162

1. Little Jesus, sweetly sleep, do not stir;
   we will lend a coat of fur;
   we will rock you, rock you, rock you,
   we will rock you, rock you, rock you,
   see the fur to keep you warm,
   snugly round your tiny form.

2. Mary's little baby sleep, sweetly sleep,
   sleep in comfort, slumber deep;
   we will rock you, rock you, rock you,
   we will rock you, rock you, rock you;
   we will serve you all we can,
   darling, darling little man.

Traditional Czech carol
trans. Percy Dearmer (1867-1936)

163

1. Lord for the years
   your love has kept and guided,
   urged and inspired us,
   cheered us on our way,
   sought us and saved us,
   pardoned and provided:
   Lord of the years,
   we bring our thanks today.

2. Lord, for that word,
   the word of life which fires us,
   speaks to our hearts
   and sets our souls ablaze,
   teaches and trains,
   rebukes us and inspires us:
   Lord of the word,
   receive your people's praise.

3. Each new disciple
   of the Crucified
   is called to bear
   the seal of him who died:

   Lift high the Cross,
   the love of Christ proclaim
   till all the world
   adore his sacred name!

4. Saved by the Cross
   whereon their Lord was slain,
   now Adam's children
   their lost home regain:

5. From north and south,
   from east and west they raise
   in growing harmony
   their song of praise:

6. O Lord, once lifted
   on the glorious tree,
   as thou hast promised,
   draw us unto thee:

7. Let ev'ry race
   and ev'ry language tell
   of him who saves
   from fear of death and hell:

8. From farthest regions,
   let them homage bring,
   and on his Cross
   adore their Saviour King:

9. Set up thy throne,
   that earth's despair may cease
   beneath the shadow
   of its healing peace:

10. For thy blest Cross
    which doth for all atone,
    creation's praises
    rise before thy throne:

11. So let the world
    proclaim with one accord
    the praises of
    our everliving Lord.

George William Kitchin (1827-1912)
and Michael Robert Newbolt (1874-1956) alt.

162

1. Little Jesus, sweetly sleep, do not stir;
   we will lend a coat of fur;
   we will rock you, rock you, rock you,
   we will rock you, rock you, rock you,
   see the fur to keep you warm,
   snugly round your tiny form.

2. Mary's little baby sleep, sweetly sleep,
   sleep in comfort, slumber deep;
   we will rock you, rock you, rock you,
   we will rock you, rock you, rock you;
   we will serve you all we can,
   darling, darling little man.

Traditional Czech carol
trans. Percy Dearmer (1867-1936)

163

1. Lord for the years
   your love has kept and guided,
   urged and inspired us,
   cheered us on our way,
   sought us and saved us,
   pardoned and provided:
   Lord of the years,
   we bring our thanks today.

2. Lord, for that word,
   the word of life which fires us,
   speaks to our hearts
   and sets our souls ablaze,
   teaches and trains,
   rebukes us and inspires us:
   Lord of the word,
   receive your people's praise.

3. Lord, for our land
in this our generation,
spirits oppressed by pleasure,
wealth and care:
for young and old,
for commonwealth and nation,
Lord of our land,
be pleased to hear our prayer.

4. Lord, for our world;
when we disown and doubt you,
loveless in strength,
and comfortless in pain,
hungry and helpless,
lost indeed without you:
Lord of the world,
we pray that Christ may reign.

5. Lord for ourselves;
in living pow'r remake us –
self on the cross
and Christ upon the throne,
past put behind us,
for the future take us:
Lord of our lives,
to live for Christ alone.

Timothy Dudley-Smith (b. 1926)

2. Lord Jesus Christ,
now and ev'ry day
teach us how to pray,
Son of God.
You have commanded us to do
this in remembrance, Lord, of you.
Into our lives your pow'r breaks
through,
living Lord.

3. Lord Jesus Christ,
you have come to us,
born as one of us,
Mary's Son.
Led out to die on Calvary,
risen from death to set us free,
living Lord Jesus, help us see
you are Lord.

4. Lord Jesus Christ,
I would come to you,
live my life for you,
Son of God.
All your commands I know are true,
your many gifts will make me new,
into my life your pow'r breaks
through,
living Lord.

Patrick Appleford (b. 1925)

164

1. Lord Jesus Christ,
you have come to us,
you are one with us,
Mary's Son;
cleansing our souls from all their sin,
pouring your love and goodness in,
Jesus, our love for you we sing,
living Lord.

165

1. Lord of our life,
and God of our salvation,
star of our night,
and hope of ev'ry nation,
hear and receive
thy Church's supplication,
Lord God almighty.

Continued overleaf

3. Lord, for our land
   in this our generation,
   spirits oppressed by pleasure,
   wealth and care:
   for young and old,
   for commonwealth and nation,
   Lord of our land,
   be pleased to hear our prayer.

4. Lord, for our world;
   when we disown and doubt you,
   loveless in strength,
   and comfortless in pain,
   hungry and helpless,
   lost indeed without you:
   Lord of the world,
   we pray that Christ may reign.

5. Lord for ourselves;
   in living pow'r remake us –
   self on the cross
   and Christ upon the throne,
   past put behind us,
   for the future take us:
   Lord of our lives,
   to live for Christ alone.

   Timothy Dudley-Smith (b. 1926)

2. Lord Jesus Christ,
   now and ev'ry day
   teach us how to pray,
   Son of God.
   You have commanded us to do
   this in remembrance, Lord, of you.
   Into our lives your pow'r breaks
       through,
   living Lord.

3. Lord Jesus Christ,
   you have come to us,
   born as one of us,
   Mary's Son.
   Led out to die on Calvary,
   risen from death to set us free,
   living Lord Jesus, help us see
   you are Lord.

4. Lord Jesus Christ,
   I would come to you,
   live my life for you,
   Son of God.
   All your commands I know are true,
   your many gifts will make me new,
   into my life your pow'r breaks
       through,
   living Lord.

   Patrick Appleford (b. 1925)

164

1. Lord Jesus Christ,
   you have come to us,
   you are one with us,
   Mary's Son;
   cleansing our souls from all their sin,
   pouring your love and goodness in,
   Jesus, our love for you we sing,
   living Lord.

165

1. Lord of our life,
   and God of our salvation,
   star of our night,
   and hope of ev'ry nation,
   hear and receive
   thy Church's supplication,
   Lord God almighty.

   Continued overleaf

2. Lord, thou canst help
   when earthly armour faileth,
   Lord, thou canst save
   when deadly sin assaileth;
   Christ, o'er thy rock
   nor death nor hell prevaileth;
   grant us thy peace, Lord.

3. Peace in our hearts,
   our evil thoughts assuaging;
   peace in thy Church,
   where people are engaging;
   peace, when the world
   its busy war is waging:
   calm all our raging.

4. Grant us thy grace
   through trial and temptation,
   grant us thy truth,
   thy promise of salvation,
   grant us thy peace
   in ev'ry heart and nation,
   and in thy heaven.

Philip Pusey (1799-1855) based on the German of
Matthäus Apelles von Löwenstern (1594-1648) alt.

166

1. Lord, the light of your love is shining,
   in the midst of the darkness, shining;
   Jesus, Light of the World,
      shine upon us,
   set us free by the truth
   you now bring us,
   shine on me, shine on me.

   Shine, Jesus, shine,
   fill this land with the Father's glory;
   blaze, Spirit, blaze,
   set our hearts on fire.
   Flow, river, flow,
   flood the nations with grace and mercy;
   send forth your Word, Lord,
   and let there be light.

2. Lord, I come to your
      awesome presence,
   from the shadows into your radiance;
   by the blood I may enter
      your brightness,
   search me, try me, consume
   all my darkness.
   Shine on me, shine on me.

3. As we gaze on your kingly brightness
   so our faces display your likeness,
   ever changing from glory to glory,
   mirrored here may our lives
   tell your story.
   Shine on me, shine on me.

   Graham Kendrick (b. 1950)
   © 1987 Make Way Music Ltd

167

1. Lord, we come to ask your healing,
   teach us of love;
   all unspoken shame revealing,
   teach us of love.
   Take our selfish thoughts and actions,
   petty feuds, divisive factions,
   hear us now to you appealing,
   teach us of love.

2. Soothe away our pain and sorrow,
   hold us in love;
   grace we cannot buy or borrow,
   hold us in love.
   Though we see but dark and danger,
   though we spurn both friend and
      stranger,
   though we often dread tomorrow,
   hold us in love.

3. When the bread is raised and broken,
   fill us with love;
   words of consecration spoken,
   fill us with love.
   As our grateful prayers continue,
   make the faith that we have in you
   more than just an empty token,
   fill us with love.

4. Help us live for one another,
   bind us in love;
   stranger, neighbour, father, mother –
   bind us in love.
   All are equal at your table,
   through your Spirit make us able
   to embrace as sister, brother,
   bind us in love.

   Jean Holloway (b. 1939)

168

1. Love came down at Christmas,
   Love all lovely, Love divine;
   Love was born at Christmas,
   star and angels gave the sign.

2. Worship we the Godhead,
   Love incarnate, Love divine;
   worship we our Jesus:
   but wherewith for sacred sign?

3. Love shall be our token,
   love be yours and love be mine,
   love to God and all men,
   love for plea and gift and sign.

   Christina Georgina Rossetti (1830-1894)

169

1. Love is his word, love is his way,
   feasting with all, fasting alone,
   living and dying, rising again,
   love, only love, is his way.

   *Richer than gold is the love of my
   Lord:
   better than splendour and wealth.*

2. Love is his way, love is his mark,
   sharing his last Passover feast,
   Christ at the table, host to the twelve,
   love, only love, is his mark.

3. Love is his mark, love is his sign,
   bread for our strength, wine for our
   joy,
   'This is my body, this is my blood.'
   Love, only love, is his sign.

4. Love is his sign, love is his news,
   'Do this,' he said, 'lest you forget
   all my deep sorrow, all my dear blood.'
   Love, only love, is his news.

5. Love is his news, love is his name,
   we are his own, chosen and called,
   family, brethren, cousins and kin.
   Love, only love, is his name.

6. Love is his name, love is his law,
   hear his command, all who are his,
   'Love one another, I have loved you.'
   Love, only love, is his law.

7. Love is his law, love is his word:
   love of the Lord, Father and Word,
   love of the Spirit, God ever one,
   love, only love, is his word.

   Luke Connaughton (1917-1979) alt.

170

1. Loving Shepherd of thy sheep,
   keep thy lamb, in safety keep;
   nothing can thy pow'r withstand,
   none can pluck me from thy hand.

2. Loving Shepherd, thou didst give
   thine own life that we might live;
   and the hands outstretched to bless
   bear the cruel nails' impress.

3. I would praise thee ev'ry day,
   gladly all thy will obey,
   like thy blessèd ones above
   happy in thy precious love.

4. Loving Shepherd, ever near,
   teach thy lamb thy voice to hear;
   suffer not my steps to stray
   from the straight and narrow way.

5. Where thou leadest I would go,
   walking in thy steps below;
   then, before my Father's throne,
   I shall know as I am known.

Jane Elizabeth Leeson (1809-1881)

171

1. Low in the grave he lay,
   Jesus, my Saviour;
   waiting the coming day,
   Jesus, my Lord.

   *Up from the grave he arose,
   with a mighty triumph o'er his foes;
   he arose a victor
   from the dark domain,
   and he lives for ever
   with his saints to reign.
   He arose! He arose!
   Hallelujah! Christ arose!*

2. Vainly they watch his bed,
   Jesus, my Saviour;
   vainly they seal the dead,
   Jesus, my Lord.

3. Death cannot keep its prey,
   Jesus, my Saviour;
   he tore the bars away,
   Jesus, my Lord.

Robert Lowry (1826-1899)

172

Majesty, worship his majesty;
unto Jesus be glory,
honour and praise.
Majesty, kingdom, authority
flow from his throne unto his own:
his anthem raise.
So exalt, lift up on high
the name of Jesus;
magnify, come glorify
Christ Jesus the King.
Majesty, worship his majesty,
Jesus who died, now glorified,
King of all kings.

Jack W. Hayford (b. 1934)

173

1. Make me a channel of your peace.
   Where there is hatred,
   let me bring your love.
   Where there is injury,
   your pardon, Lord,
   and where there's doubt,
   true faith in you.

O Master, grant that I may never seek
so much to be consoled as to console,
to be understood, as to understand,
to be loved, as to love with all my soul.

2. Make me a channel of your peace.
   Where there's despair in life,
   let me bring hope.
   Where there is darkness,
   only light,
   and where there's sadness,
   ever joy.

3. Make me a channel of your peace.
   It is in pardoning
   that we are pardoned,
   in giving of ourselves
   that we receive,
   and in dying
   that we're born to eternal life.

The Refrain is not sung after this verse.

Sebastian Temple (b. 1928)
based on the Prayer of St. Francis
© 1967 OCP Publications

174

1. Make way, make way,
   for Christ the King in splendour
     arrives;
   fling wide the gates
   and welcome him into your lives.

   Make way, make way,
   for the King of kings;
   make way, make way,
   and let his kingdom in!

2. He comes the broken hearts to heal,
   the pris'ners to free;
   the deaf shall hear, the lame shall
     dance,
   the blind shall see.

3. And those who mourn with heavy
     hearts,
   who weep and sigh,
   with laughter, joy and royal crown
   he'll beautify.

4. We call you now to worship him
   as Lord of all,
   to have no gods before him,
   their thrones must fall!

Graham Kendrick (b. 1950)
© 1986 Make Way Music

175

1. Man of sorrows! What a name
   for the Son of God who came
   ruined sinners to reclaim!
   Alleluia! What a Saviour!

2. Bearing shame and scoffing rude,
   in my place condemned he stood;
   sealed my pardon with his blood;
   Alleluia! What a Saviour!

3. Guilty, vile and helpless we;
   spotless Lamb of God was he:
   full atonement – can it be?
   Alleluia! What a Saviour!

4. Lifted up was he to die:
   'It is finished!' was his cry;
   now in heav'n exalted high;
   Alleluia! What a Saviour!

5. When he comes, our glorious King,
   all his ransomed home to bring,
   then anew this song we'll sing:
   Alleluia! what a Saviour!

Philipp Bliss (1838-1876) alt.

176

1. Mary, blessed grieving mother,
   waiting by the cross of shame,
   through your patient, prayerful vigil,
   kindle hope's eternal flame;
   crying in the pains of earth,
   singing of redemption's birth.

2. Where the crosses of the nations
   darken still the noon-day skies,
   see the sad madonna weeping
   through a million mothers' eyes.
   Holy Mary, full of grace,
   all our tears with yours embrace.

3. Standing with the suff'ring Saviour,
   still oppressed by hate and fear,
   where the gentle still are murdered
   and protestors disappear:
   mother of the crucified,
   call his people to your side!

4. Holy mother, watching, waiting,
   for the saving of the earth;
   in the loneliness of dying,
   speak of hope and human worth,
   there for all the world to see,
   lifted up at Calvary!

   Michael Forster (b. 1946)

177

1. Mary, blessed teenage mother,
   with what holy joy you sing!
   Humble, yet above all other,
   from your womb shall healing spring.
   Out of wedlock pregnant found,
   full of grace with blessing crowned.

2. Mother of the homeless stranger
   only outcasts recognise,
   point us to the modern manger;
   not a sight for gentle eyes!
   O the joyful news we tell:
   'Even here, Immanuel!'

3. Now, throughout the townships
       ringing,
   hear the black madonna cry,
   songs of hope and freedom singing,
   poor and humble lifted high.
   Here the Spirit finds a womb
   for the breaker of the tomb!

4. Holy mother, for the nations
   bring to birth the child divine:
   Israel's strength and consolation,
   and the hope of Palestine!
   All creation reconciled
   in the crying of a child!

   Michael Forster (b. 1946)

178

1. May the mind of Christ my Saviour
   live in me from day to day,
   by his love and pow'r controlling
   all I do and say.

2. May the word of God dwell richly
   in my heart from hour to hour,
   so that I may triumph only
   in his saving pow'r.

3. May the peace of God my Father
   rule my life in ev'rything,
   that I may be calm to comfort
   sick and sorrowing.

4. May the love of Jesus fill me,
   as the waters fill the sea;
   him exalting, self abasing,
   this is victory.

5. May I run the race before me,
   strong and brave to face the foe,
   looking only unto Jesus,
   as I onward go.

   Kate Barclay Wilkinson (1859-1928)

3. Wisdom unsearchable,
   God the invisible;
   love indestructible
   in frailty appears.
   Lord of infinity,
   stooping so tenderly,
   lifts our humanity
   to the heights of his throne.

   Graham Kendrick (b. 1950)
   © 1986 Kingsway's Thankyou Music

179

1. Meekness and majesty,
   manhood and deity,
   in perfect harmony,
   the man who is God.
   Lord of eternity
   dwells in humanity,
   kneels in humility
   and washes our feet.

   O, what a mystery,
   meekness and majesty,
   bow down and worship,
   for this is your God.
   This is your God.

2. Father's pure radiance,
   perfect in innocence,
   yet learns obedience
   to death on a cross.
   Suff'ring to give us life,
   conqu'ring through sacrifice;
   and as they crucify
   prays: 'Father forgive'.

180

1. Morning has broken
   like the first morning;
   blackbird has spoken
   like the first bird.
   Praise for the singing!
   Praise for the morning!
   Praise for them, springing
   fresh from the Word!

2. Sweet the rain's new fall,
   sunlit from heaven,
   like the first dew-fall
   on the first grass.
   Praise for the sweetness
   of the wet garden,
   sprung from completeness
   where his feet pass.

3. Mine is the sunlight!
   Mine is the morning
   born of the one light
   Eden saw play!
   Praise with elation,
   praise ev'ry morning,
   God's re-creation
   of the new day!

   Eleanor Farjeon (1881-1965)

181

1. 'Moses, I know you're the man,'
the Lord said.
'You're going to work out my plan,'
the Lord said.
'Lead all the Israelites
out of slavery,
and I shall make them a
wandering race
called the people of God.'

So ev'ry day
we're on our way,
for we're a travelling, wandering race
called the people of God.

2. 'Don't get too set in your ways,'
the Lord said.
'Each step is only a phase,'
the Lord said.
'I'll go before you and
I shall be a sign
to guide my travelling,
wandering race.
You're the people of God.'

3. 'No matter what you may do,'
the Lord said,
'I shall be faithful and true,'
the Lord said.
'My love will strengthen you
as you go along,
for you're my travelling,
wandering race.
You're the people of God.'

4. 'Look at the birds in the air,'
the Lord said.
'They fly unhampered by care,'
the Lord said.
'You will move easier
if you're travelling light,
for you're a wandering,
vagabond race.
You're the people of God.'

5. 'Foxes have places to go,'
the Lord said,
'but I've no home here below,'
the Lord said.
'So if you want to be with me
all your days,
keep up the moving
and travelling on.
You're the people of God.'

Estelle White (b. 1925)

182

1. My faith looks up to thee,
thou Lamb of Calvary,
Saviour divine!
Now hear me while I pray,
take all my guilt away,
O let me from this day
be wholly thine.

2. May thy rich grace impart
strength to my fainting heart,
my zeal inspire.
As thou hast died for me,
O may my love to thee
pure, warm and changeless be,
a living fire.

3. While life's dark maze I tread,
and griefs around me spread,
be thou my guide;
bid darkness turn to day,
wipe sorrow's tears away,
nor let me ever stray
from thee aside.

4. When ends life's transient dream,
when death's cold sullen stream
shall o'er me roll,
blest Saviour, then in love,
fear and distrust remove;
O bear me safe above,
a ransomed soul.

Ray Palmer (1808-1887)

183

1. My Father, for another night
of quiet sleep and rest,
for all the joy of morning light,
thy holy name be blest.

2. Now with the new-born day I give
myself anew to thee,
that as thou willest I may live,
and what thou willest be.

3. Whate'er I do, things great or small,
whate'er I speak or frame,
thy glory may I seek in all,
do all in Jesus' name.

4. My Father, for his sake, I pray,
thy child accept and bless;
and lead me by thy grace today
in paths of righteousness.

Henry Williams Baker (1821-1877)

184

1. My God, accept my heart this day,
and make it always thine,
that I from thee no more may stray,
no more from thee decline.

2. Before the cross of him who died,
behold, I prostrate fall;
let ev'ry sin be crucified,
and Christ be all in all.

3. Anoint me with thy heav'nly grace,
and seal me for thine own;
that I may see thy glorious face,
and worship near thy throne.

4. Let ev'ry thought and work and word
to thee be ever giv'n:
then life shall be thy service, Lord,
and death the gate of heav'n.

5. All glory to the Father be,
all glory to the Son,
all glory, Holy Ghost, to thee,
while endless ages run.

Matthew Bridges (1800-1894)

185

1. My Lord, what love is this
that pays so dearly,
that I, the guilty one,
may go free!

*Amazing love,
O what sacrifice,
the Son of God giv'n for me.
My debt he pays and my death he dies,
that I might live, that I might live.*

Continued overleaf

2. And so they watched him die,
   despised, rejected;
   but oh, the blood he shed
   flowed for me!

   Amazing love,
   O what sacrifice,
   the Son of God giv'n for me.
   My debt he pays and my death he dies,
   that I might live, that I might live.

3. And now this love of Christ
   shall flow like rivers;
   come wash your guilt away,
   live again!

Graham Kendrick (b. 1950)
© 1989 Make Way Music Ltd

186

Spanish text

Nada te turbe,
nada te espante.
Quien a Dios tiene
nada le falta.
Nada te turbe,
nada te espante.
Solo Dios basta.

English text

Nothing can trouble,
nothing can frighten.
Those who seek God shall
never go wanting.
Nothing can trouble,
nothing can frighten.
God alone fills us.

St. Teresa of Avila

187

1. Nearer, my God, to thee,
   nearer to thee!
   E'en though it be a cross
   that raiseth me:
   still all my song would be,
   'Nearer, my God, to thee,
   nearer to thee.'

2. Though, like the wanderer,
   the sun gone down,
   darkness be over me,
   my rest a stone;
   yet in my dreams I'd be
   nearer, my God, to thee,
   nearer to thee!

3. There let the way appear,
   steps unto heav'n;
   all that thou sendest me
   in mercy giv'n:
   angels to beckon me
   nearer, my God, to thee,
   nearer to thee!

4. Then, with my waking thoughts
   bright with thy praise,
   out of my stony griefs
   Bethel I'll raise;
   so by my woes to be
   nearer, my God, to thee,
   nearer to thee!

5. Or if on joyful wing
   cleaving the sky,
   sun, moon and stars forgot,
   upwards I fly,
   still all my song shall be,
   'Nearer, my God, to thee,
   nearer to thee.'

Sarah Flower Adams (1805-1848)

188

1. New songs of celebration render
   to him who has great wonders done.
   Love sits enthroned in ageless
      splendour:
   come and adore the mighty one.
   He has made known his great salvation
   which all his friends with joy confess:
   he has revealed to ev'ry nation
   his everlasting righteousness.

2. Joyfully, heartily resounding,
   let ev'ry instrument and voice
   peal out the praise of grace abounding,
   calling the whole world to rejoice.
   Trumpets and organs, set in motion
   such sounds as make the heavens ring;
   all things that live in earth and ocean,
   make music for your mighty King.

3. Rivers and seas and torrents roaring,
   honour the Lord with wild acclaim;
   mountains and stones look up adoring
   and find a voice to praise his name.
   Righteous, commanding, ever glorious,
   praises be his that never cease:
   just is our God, whose truth victorious
   establishes the world in peace.

   Erik Routley (1917-1982)
   © 1974 Hope Publishing Co

189

1. O Breath of Life,
   come sweeping through us,
   revive your Church with life and pow'r;
   O Breath of Life, come cleanse,
      renew us,
   and fit your Church to meet this hour.

2. O Breath of Love,
   come breathe within us,
   renewing thought and will and heart;
   come, love of Christ, afresh to win us,
   revive your Church in ev'ry part!

3. O Wind of God,
   come bend us, break us,
   till humbly we confess our need;
   then, in your tenderness remake us,
   revive, restore – for this we plead.

4. Revive us, Lord;
   is zeal abating
   while harvest fields are vast and white?
   Revive us, Lord, the world is waiting –
   equip thy Church to spread the light.

   Elizabeth Ann Porter Head (1850-1936)

190

1. O God beyond all praising,
   we worship you today,
   and sing the love amazing
   that songs cannot repay;
   for we can only wonder
   at ev'ry gift you send,
   at blessings without number
   and mercies without end:
   we lift our hearts before you
   and wait upon your word,
   we honour and adore you,
   our great and mighty Lord.

   Continued overleaf

2. Then hear, O gracious Saviour,
   accept the love we bring,
   that we who know your favour
   may serve you as our king;
   and whether our tomorrows
   be filled with good or ill,
   we'll triumph through our sorrows
   and rise to bless you still:
   to marvel at your beauty
   and glory in your ways,
   and make a joyful duty
   our sacrifice of praise.

   Michael Perry (b. 1942)

191

1. O God of earth and altar,
   bow down and hear our cry,
   our earthly rulers falter,
   our people drift and die;
   the walls of gold entomb us,
   the swords of scorn divide,
   take not thy thunder from us,
   but take away our pride.

2. From all that terror teaches,
   from lies of tongue and pen,
   from all the easy speeches
   that comfort cruel men,
   from sale and profanation
   of honour and the sword,
   from sleep and from damnation,
   deliver us, good Lord!

3. Tie in a living tether
   the prince and priest and thrall,
   bind all our lives together,
   smite us and save us all;
   in ire and exultation
   aflame with faith, and free,
   lift up a living nation,
   a single sword to thee.

   Gilbert Keith Chesterton (1874-1936)

192

1. O happy day! that fixed my choice
   on thee, my Saviour and my God!
   Well may this glowing heart rejoice,
   and tell its raptures all abroad.

2. 'Tis done, the work of grace is done!
   I am my Lord's, and he is mine!
   He drew me, and I followed on,
   glad to confess the voice divine.

3. Now rest, my long-divided heart,
   fixed on this blissful centre, rest;
   nor ever from thy Lord depart,
   with him of ev'ry good possessed.

4. High heav'n, that heard the solemn vow,
   that vow renewed shall daily hear;
   till in life's latest hour I bow,
   and bless in death a bond so dear.

*When a tune with a Refrain is used this is
sung after each verse:*

   *O happy day! O happy day!
   When Jesus washed my sins away;
   he taught me how to watch and pray,
   and live rejoicing ev'ry day;
   O happy day! O happy day!
   When Jesus washed my sins away.*

   Philip Doddridge (1702-1751) alt.

193

1. O Lamb of God, most holy,
   salvation's perfect sign,
   by your redeeming passion,
   we share the life divine.
   The cost of our deliv'rance
   in flowing blood is shown,
   and life in all its fullness
   is found in you alone.

2. Upon the cross you carried
   a universe of shame,
   your dying breath atoning
   for centuries of blame.
   So now accept your servant,
   who on your love relied,
   to rest in peace eternal,
   redeemed and purified.

3. O draw us to your presence,
   beyond the sundered veil,
   to stand in silent wonder,
   where words and senses fail.
   In fellowship unbroken
   with all who went before,
   we join with saints and angels
   to worship and adore.

Michael Forster (b. 1946) based on the German

194

1. O let the Son of God enfold you
   with his Spirit and his love,
   let him fill your heart
   and satisfy your soul.
   O let him have the things that
     hold you,
   and his Spirit, like a dove,
   will descend upon your life
     and make you whole.

Jesus, O Jesus,
come and fill your lambs.
Jesus, O Jesus,
come and fill your lambs.

2. O come and sing this song with
     gladness
   as your hearts are filled with joy;
   lift your hands in sweet
   surrender to his name.
   O give him all your tears and sadness,
   give him all your years of pain,
   and you'll enter into life in Jesus' name.

John Wimber (b. 1933)
© *1979 Mercy/Vineyard Publishing/Integrity's Hosanna! Music*

195

1. O little one sweet,
   O little one mild,
   thy Father's purpose thou hast fulfilled;
   thou cam'st from heav'n
   to dwell below,
   to share the joys and tears we know.
   O little one sweet,
   O little one mild.

2. O little one sweet,
   O little one mild,
   with joy thou hast the whole world
     filled;
   thou camest here
   from heav'n's domain,
   to bring us comfort in our pain,
   O little one sweet,
   O little one mild.

3. O little one sweet,
   O little one mild,
   in thee Love's beauties are all distilled;
   then light in us
   thy love's bright flame,
   that we may give thee back the same,
   O little one sweet,
   O little one mild.

German, Samuel Scheidt (1650)
trans. Percy Dearmer (1867-1936) alt.

196

1. O Lord, all the world
   belongs to you,
   and you are always
   making all things new.
   What is wrong you forgive,
   and the new life you give
   is what's turning
   the world upside down.

2. The world's only
   loving to its friends,
   but you have brought us
   love that never ends;
   loving enemies too,
   and this loving with you
   is what's turning the world upside down.

3. This world lives divided
   and apart.
   You draw us all together
   and we start,
   in your body, to see
   that in fellowship we
   can be turning the world upside down.

4. The world wants the wealth
   to live in state,
   but you show us a new way
   to be great:
   like a servant you came,
   and if we do the same,
   we'll be turning the world upside down.

5. O Lord, all the world
   belongs to you,
   and you are always
   making all things new.
   Send your Spirit on all
   in your Church whom you call
   to be turning the world upside down.

Patrick Appleford (b. 1925) alt.

197

O Lord, hear my prayer,
O Lord, hear my prayer:
when I call, answer me.
O Lord, hear my prayer,
O Lord, hear my prayer.
Come and listen to me.

Taizé

198

1. O Lord, my God,
   when I, in awesome wonder,
   consider all the works
   thy hand has made,
   I see the stars,
   I hear the rolling thunder,
   thy pow'r throughout
   the universe displayed.

   Then sings my soul,
   my Saviour God, to thee:
   how great thou art,
   how great thou art.
   Then sings my soul,
   my Saviour God, to thee:
   how great thou art,
   how great thou art.

2. When through the woods
   and forest glades I wander,
   and hear the birds
   sing sweetly in the trees;
   when I look down
   from lofty mountain grandeur,
   and hear the brook,
   and feel the gentle breeze.

3. And when I think that God,
   his Son not sparing,
   sent him to die,
   I scarce can take it in
   that on the cross,
   my burden gladly bearing,
   he bled and died
   to take away my sin.

4. When Christ shall come
   with shout of acclamation,
   and take me home,
   what joy shall fill my heart;
   then I shall bow
   in humble adoration,
   and there proclaim:
   my God, how great thou art.

Karl Boberg (1859-1940)
trans. Stuart K. Hine (1899-1989)
© *1953 Stuart K. Hine/Kingsway's Thankyou Music*

199

1. O Lord of our salvation,
   the pains of all creation
   are borne upon your cross:
   the failure of compassion,
   revealed in starkest fashion,
   exposes all our gold as dross.

2. We hear your voice protesting,
   to love and hope attesting,
   where justice is denied.
   Where innocents are dying,
   where hate is crucifying,
   you call us to your bleeding side.

3. O give us faith to stay here,
   to wait, to watch and pray here,
   and witness to your cry;
   in scarred and tearful faces,
   in countless painful places,
   you give us hope that will not die.

Michael Forster (b. 1946)

200

O Lord, your tenderness,
melting all my bitterness,
O Lord, I receive your love.
O Lord, your loveliness,
changing all my ugliness,
O Lord, I receive your love.
O Lord, I receive your love.
O Lord, I receive your love.

Graham Kendrick (b. 1950)
© *1986 Kingsway's Thankyou Music*

201

1. O Love that wilt not let me go,
   I rest my weary soul in thee;
   I give thee back the life I owe,
   that in thine ocean depths its flow
   may richer, fuller be.

2. O Light that follow'st all my way,
   I yield my flick'ring torch to thee;
   my heart restores its borrowed ray,
   that in thy sunshine's blaze its day
   may brighter, fairer be.

3. O Joy that seekest me through pain,
   I cannot close my heart to thee;
   I trace the rainbow through the rain,
   and feel the promise is not vain
   that morn shall tearless be.

4. O Cross that liftest up my head,
   I dare not ask to fly from thee:
   I lay in dust life's glory dead,
   and from the ground there blossoms
   red
   life that shall endless be.

George Matheson (1842-1906)

202

1. O my Saviour, lifted
   from the earth for me,
   draw me, in thy mercy,
   nearer unto thee.

2. Lift my earth-bound longings,
   fix them, Lord, above;
   draw me with the magnet
   of thy mighty love.

3. Lord, thine arms are stretching
   ever far and wide,
   to enfold thy children
   to thy loving side.

4. And I come, O Jesus:
   dare I turn away?
   No, thy love hath conquered,
   and I come today.

5. Bringing all my burdens,
   sorrow, sin and care;
   at thy feet I lay them,
   and I leave them there.

William Walsham How (1823-1897)

203

Oh! Oh! Oh! how good is the Lord,
Oh! Oh! Oh! how good is the Lord,
Oh! Oh! Oh! how good is the Lord,
I never will forget
what he has done for me.

1. He gives me salvation,
   how good is the Lord,
   he gives me salvation,
   how good is the Lord,
   he gives me salvation,
   how good is the Lord,
   I never will forget
   what he has done for me.

2. He gives me his blessings . . .

3. He gives me his Spirit . . .

4. He gives me his healing . . .

5. He gives me his glory . . .

Other verses may be added, as appropriate

Unknown

204

1. On a hill far away
   stood an old rugged cross,
   the emblem of suff'ring and shame;
   and I loved that old cross
   where the dearest and best
   for a world of lost sinners was slain.

   So I'll cherish the old rugged cross,
   till my trophies at last I lay down;
   I will cling to the old rugged cross
   and exchange it some day for a crown.

2. O, that old rugged cross,
   so despised by the world,
   has a wondrous attraction for me:
   for the dear Lamb of God
   left his glory above
   to bear it to dark Calvary.

3. In the old rugged cross,
   stained with blood so divine,
   a wondrous beauty I see.
   For 'twas on that old cross
   Jesus suffered and died
   to pardon and sanctify me.

4. To the old rugged cross
   I will ever be true,
   its shame and reproach gladly bear.
   Then he'll call me some day
   to my home far away;
   there his glory for ever I'll share.

George Bennard (1873-1958)
© The Rodeheaver Co/Word Music Inc/
Word Music (UK)/CopyCare Ltd

205

1. On Christmas night all Christians sing,
   to hear the news the angels bring,
   on Christmas night all Christians sing,
   to hear the news the angels bring,
   news of great joy, news of great mirth,
   news of our merciful King's birth.

2. Then why should we on earth be
      so sad,
   since our Redeemer made us glad,
   then why should we on earth be
      so sad,
   since our Redeemer made us glad,
   when from our sin he set us free,
   all for to gain our liberty?

3. When sin departs before his grace,
   then life and health come in its place,
   when sin departs before his grace,
   then life and health come in its place,
   angels and earth with joy may sing,
   all for to see the new-born King.

4. All out of darkness we have light,
   which made the angels sing this night:
   all out of darkness we have light,
   which made the angels sing this night:
   'Glory to God and peace to men,
   now and for evermore. Amen.'

Traditional English carol alt.

206

1. On this day, the first of days,
   God the Father's name we praise,
   who, creation's Lord and spring,
   did the world from darkness bring.

2. On this day his only Son
   over death the triumph won;
   on this day the Spirit came
   with his gifts of living flame.

3. On this day his people raise
   one pure sacrifice of praise,
   and, with all the saints above,
   tell of Christ's redeeming love.

4. Praise, O God, to thee be giv'n,
   praise on earth and praise in heav'n,
   praise to thy eternal Son,
   who this day our vict'ry won.

18th century trans. Henry Williams Baker (1821-
1877) adapted by the editors of 'English Praise'

207

1. One more step along the world I go,
   one more step along the world I go.
   From the old things to the new
   keep me travelling along with you.

   And it's from the old
   I travel to the new,
   keep me travelling
   along with you.

2. Round the corners of the world I turn,
   more and more about the world
      I learn.
   All the new things that I see
   you'll be looking at along with me.

Continued overleaf

3. As I travel through the bad and good,
   keep me travelling the way I should.
   Where I see no way to go,
   you'll be telling me the way, I know.

   And it's from the old
   I travel to the new,
   keep me travelling
   along with you.

4. Give me courage when the world
      is rough,
   keep me loving though the world
      is tough.
   Leap and sing in all I do,
   keep me travelling along with you.

5. You are older than the world can be,
   you are younger than the life in me.
   Ever old and ever new,
   keep me travelling along with you.

   Sydney Carter (b. 1915)

208

1. One shall tell another,
   and all shall tell their friends,
   husbands, wives and children
   shall come following on.
   From house to house in fam'lies
   shall more be gathered in;
   and lights will shine in ev'ry street,
   so warm and welcoming.

   Come on in and taste the new wine,
   the wine of the kingdom,
   the wine of the kingdom of God:
   here is healing and forgiveness,
   the wine of the kingdom,
   the wine of the kingdom of God.

2. Compassion of the Father
   is ready now to flow;
   through acts of love and mercy
   we must let it show.
   He turns now from his anger
   to show a smiling face,
   and longs that all should stand beneath
   the fountain of his grace.

3. He longs to do much more than
   our faith has yet allowed,
   to thrill us and surprise us
   with his sov'reign pow'r.
   Where darkness has been darkest,
   the brightest light will shine;
   his invitation comes to us –
   it's yours and it is mine.

   Graham Kendrick (b. 1950)
   © 1981 Kingsway's Thankyou Music

209

1. Only by grace can we enter,
   only by grace can we stand;
   not by our human endeavour,
   but by the blood of the Lamb.
   Into your presence you call us,
   you call us to come.
   Into your presence you draw us,
   and now by your grace we come,
   now by your grace we come.

2. Lord, if you mark our transgressions,
   who would stand?
   Thanks to your grace we are cleansed
   by the blood of the Lamb.
   Lord, if you mark our transgressions,
   who would stand?
   Thanks to your grace we are cleansed
   by the blood of the Lamb.

Repeat verse 1

   Gerrit Gustafson
   © 1990 Integrity's Hosanna! Music/
   Kingsway's Thankyou Music

210

1. Onward, Christian pilgrims,
   Christ will be our light;
   see, the heav'nly vision
   breaks upon our sight!
   Out of death's enslavement
   Christ has set us free,
   on then to salvation,
   hope and liberty.

   Onward, Christian pilgrims,
   Christ will be our light;
   see, the heav'nly vision
   breaks upon our sight!

2. Onward, Christian pilgrims,
   up the rocky way,
   where the dying Saviour
   bids us watch and pray.
   Through the darkened valley
   walk with those who mourn,
   share the pain and anger,
   share the promised dawn!

3. Onward, Christian pilgrims,
   in the early dawn;
   death's great seal is broken,
   life and hope reborn!
   Faith in resurrection
   strengthens pilgrims' hearts,
   ev'ry load is lightened,
   ev'ry fear departs.

4. Onward, Christian pilgrims,
   hearts and voices raise,
   till the whole creation
   echoes perfect praise:
   swords are turned to ploughshares,
   pride and envy cease,
   truth embraces justice,
   hope resolves in peace.

   Michael Forster (b. 1946)

211

Open our eyes, Lord,
we want to see Jesus,
to reach out and touch him
and say that we love him;
open our ears, Lord,
and help us to listen;
O, open our eyes, Lord,
we want to see Jesus!

Robert Cull (b. 1949)

212

1. Our Father, who art in heaven,
   hallowèd be thy name.
   Thy kingdom come, thy will be done,
   hallowèd be thy name,
   hallowèd be thy name.

2. On earth as it is in heaven.
   Give us this day our daily bread.

3. Forgive us our trespasses,
   as we forgive those who trespass
     against us.

4. Lead us not into temptation,
   but deliver us from all that is evil.

5. For thine is the kingdom, the power
     and the glory,
   for ever and for ever and ever.

6. Amen, amen, it shall be so.
   Amen, amen, it shall be so.

   Traditional Caribbean,
   based on Matthew 6:9-13 and Luke 11:2-4

213

1. Peace is flowing like a river,
   flowing out through you and me,
   spreading out into the desert,
   setting all the captives free.

   Let it flow through me,
   let it flow through me,
   let the mighty peace of God
   flow out through me.
   Let it flow through me,
   let it flow through me,
   let the mighty peace of God
   flow out through me.

2. Love is flowing like a river,
   flowing out through you and me,
   spreading out into the desert,
   setting all the captives free.

3. Joy is flowing like a river,
   flowing out through you and me,
   spreading out into the desert,
   setting all the captives free.

4. Faith is flowing like a river,
   flowing out through you and me,
   spreading out into the desert,
   setting all the captives free.

5. Hope is flowing like a river,
   flowing out through you and me,
   spreading out into the desert,
   setting all the captives free.

   Unknown

214

1. Peace, perfect peace,
   in this dark world of sin?
   The blood of Jesus
   whispers peace within.

2. Peace, perfect peace,
   by thronging duties pressed?
   To do the will of Jesus,
   this is rest.

3. Peace, perfect peace,
   with sorrows surging round?
   In Jesus' presence
   naught but calm is found.

4. Peace, perfect peace,
   with loved ones far away?
   In Jesus' keeping
   we are safe, and they.

5. Peace, perfect peace,
   our future all unknown?
   Jesus we know,
   and he is on the throne.

6. Peace, perfect peace,
   death shad'wing us and ours?
   Jesus has vanquished death
   and all its pow'rs.

7. It is enough: earth's struggles
   soon shall cease,
   and Jesus call us
   to heav'n's perfect peace.

   Edward Henry Bickersteth (1825-1906)

215

1. Peace, perfect peace,
   is the gift of Christ our Lord.
   Peace, perfect peace,
   is the gift of Christ our Lord.
   Thus, says the Lord,
   will the world know my friends.
   Peace, perfect peace,
   is the gift of Christ our Lord.

2. Love, perfect love,
   is the gift of Christ our Lord.
   Love, perfect love,
   is the gift of Christ our Lord.
   Thus, says the Lord,
   will the world know my friends.
   Love, perfect love,
   is the gift of Christ our Lord.

3. Faith, perfect faith,
   is the gift of Christ our Lord.
   Faith, perfect faith,
   is the gift of Christ our Lord.
   Thus, says the Lord,
   will the world know my friends.
   Faith, perfect faith,
   is the gift of Christ our Lord.

4. Hope, perfect hope,
   is the gift of Christ our Lord.
   Hope, perfect hope,
   is the gift of Christ our Lord.
   Thus, says the Lord,
   will the world know my friends.
   Hope, perfect hope,
   is the gift of Christ our Lord.

5. Joy, perfect joy,
   is the gift of Christ our Lord.
   Joy, perfect joy,
   is the gift of Christ our Lord.
   Thus, says the Lord,
   will the world know my friends.
   Joy, perfect joy,
   is the gift of Christ our Lord.

Kevin Mayhew (b. 1942)

216

Peace to you.
We bless you now
in the name of the Lord.
Peace to you.
We bless you now
in the name of the Prince of Peace.
Peace to you.

Graham Kendrick (b. 1950)
© 1988 Make Way Music Ltd

217

Peter and John went to pray,
they met a lame man on the way.
He asked for alms
and held out his palms
and this is what Peter did say:
'Silver and gold have I none,
but such as I have give I thee,
in the name of Jesus Christ
of Nazareth, rise up and walk!'
He went walking and leaping
and praising God,
walking and leaping
and praising God.
'In the name of Jesus Christ
of Nazareth, rise up and walk.'

Unknown, based on Acts 3

218

Praise God from whom all blessings flow,
praise him, all creatures here below,
praise him above ye heav'nly host,
praise Father, Son and Holy Ghost.

Thomas Ken (1637-1710)

219

Praise him on the trumpet,
the psalt'ry and harp;
praise him on the timbrel and the dance;
praise him with stringed instruments too;
praise him on the loud cymbals,
praise him on the loud cymbals;
let ev'rything that has breath praise the
    Lord!

Hallelujah, praise the Lord;
hallelujah, praise the Lord:
let ev'rything that has breath
praise the Lord!
Hallelujah, praise the Lord;
hallelujah, praise the Lord:
let ev'rything that has breath
praise the Lord!

John Kennett
© 1981 Kingsway's Thankyou Music

220

1. Praise him, praise him!
Jesus, our blessèd Redeemer!
Sing, O earth,
his wonderful love proclaim!
Hail him, hail him!
highest archangels in glory;
strength and honour
give to his holy name!
Like a shepherd,
Jesus will guard his children,
in his arms he carries
them all day long.

Praise him, praise him!
tell of his excellent greatness;
praise him, praise him
ever in joyful song!

2. Praise him, praise him!
Jesus, our blessèd Redeemer!
For our sins
he suffered, and bled, and died!
He – our rock,
our hope of eternal salvation,
hail him, hail him!
Jesus the crucified!
Sound his praises
– Jesus who bore our sorrows,
love unbounded, wonderful,
deep and strong.

3. Praise him, praise him!
Jesus, our blessèd Redeemer!
Heav'nly portals,
loud with hosannas ring!
Jesus, Saviour,
reigneth for ever and ever:
crown him, crown him!
Prophet, and Priest, and King!
Christ is coming,
over the world victorious,
pow'r and glory
unto the Lord belong.

Frances Jane van Alstyne
(Fanny J. Crosby) (1820-1915)

221

1. Praise him, praise him,
praise him in the morning,
praise him in the noontime.
Praise him, praise him,
praise him when the sun goes down.

2. Love him, love him,
love him in the morning,
love him in the noontime.
Love him, love him,
love him when the sun goes down.

3. Trust him, trust him,
   trust him in the morning,
   trust him in the noontime.
   Trust him, trust him,
   trust him when the sun goes down.

4. Serve him, serve him,
   serve him in the morning,
   serve him in the noontime.
   Serve him, serve him,
   serve him when the sun goes down.

5. Jesus, Jesus,
   Jesus in the morning,
   Jesus in the noontime.
   Jesus, Jesus,
   Jesus when the sun goes down.

   Unknown

222

1. Praise, O praise our God and King;
   hymns of adoration sing:

   for his mercies still endure
   ever faithful, ever sure.

2. Praise him that he made the sun
   day by day his course to run:

3. And the silver moon by night,
   shining with her gentle light:

4. Praise him that he gave the rain
   to mature the swelling grain:

5. And hath bid the fruitful field
   crops of precious increase yield:

6. Praise him for our harvest-store;
   he hath filled the garner-floor:

7. And for richer food than this,
   pledge of everlasting bliss:

8. Glory to our bounteous King;
   glory let creation sing:
   glory to the Father, Son
   and blest Spirit, Three in One.

   Henry Williams Baker (1821-1877)

223

1. Praise the Lord, rise up rejoicing,
   worship, thanks, devotion voicing:
   glory be to God on high!
   Christ, your cross and passion sharing,
   by this Eucharist declaring
   yours th'eternal victory.

2. Scattered flock, one Shepherd sharing,
   lost and lonely, one voice hearing,
   ears are open to your word;
   by your blood new life receiving,
   in your body firm, believing,
   we are yours, and you the Lord.

3. Send us forth alert and living,
   sins forgiven, wrongs forgiving,
   in your Spirit strong and free.
   Finding love in all creation,
   bringing peace in ev'ry nation,
   may we faithful foll'wers be.

   Howard Charles Adie Gaunt (1902-1983)

224

1. Purify my heart,
   let me be as gold
   and precious silver.
   Purify my heart,
   let me be as gold, pure gold.

   Refiner's fire,
   my heart's one desire
   is to be holy,
   set apart for you, Lord.
   I choose to be holy,
   set apart for you, my master,
   ready to do your will.

2. Purify my heart,
   cleanse me from within
   and make me holy.
   Purify my heart,
   cleanse me from my sin, deep within.

Brian Doerksen
© 1990 Mercy/Vineyard Publishing/Integrity's Hosanna! Music

225

1. Put thou thy trust in God,
   in duty's path go on;
   walk in his strength with faith and hope,
   so shall thy work be done.

2. Commit thy ways to him,
   thy works into his hands,
   and rest on his unchanging word,
   who heav'n and earth commands.

3. Though years on years roll on,
   his cov'nant shall endure;
   though clouds and darkness hide
      his path,
   the promised grace is sure.

4. Give to the winds thy fears;
   hope, and be undismayed:
   God hears thy sighs and counts thy
      tears;
   God shall lift up thy head.

5. Through waves and clouds and storms
   his pow'r will clear thy way:
   wait thou his time; the darkest night
   shall end in brightest day.

6. Leave to his sov'reign sway
   to choose and to command;
   so shalt thou, wond'ring, own his way,
   how wise, how strong his hand.

Paul Gerhardt (1607-1676)
trans. John Wesley (1703-1791) and others

226

Rejoice in the Lord always
and again I say rejoice.
Rejoice in the Lord always
and again I say rejoice.
Rejoice, rejoice
and again I say rejoice.
Rejoice, rejoice
and again I say rejoice.

Based on Philippians 4:4

227

1. Rejoice, the year upon its way
   has brought again that blessèd day
   when on the Church by Christ our Lord
   the Holy Spirit was outpoured.

2. From out the heav'ns a rushing noise
   came like the tempest's sudden voice,
   and mingled with th'Apostles' prayer,
   proclaiming loud that God was there.

3. Like quiv'ring tongues of light
  and flame,
upon each one the Spirit came:
tongues, that the earth might hear
  their call,
and fire, that love might burn in all.

4. And so to all were spread abroad
the wonders of the works of God;
they knew the prophet's word fulfilled,
and owned the gift which God had
  willed.

5. Look down, most gracious God,
  this day
upon thy people as we pray;
and Christ the Lord upon us pour
the Spirit's gift for evermore.
Amen.

*Based on the Latin (c. 4th century) trans. the Editors
of 'The New English Hymnal'*

3. Bend us, O Lord,
where we are hard and cold,
in your refiner's fire
come purify the gold.
Though suff'ring comes
and evil crouches near,
still our living God
is reigning, he is reigning here.

4. Restore, O Lord,
the honour of your name,
in works of sov'reign pow'r
come shake the earth again,
that all may see
and come with rev'rent fear
to the living God
whose kingdom shall outlast the years.

*Graham Kendrick (b. 1950) and Chris Rolinson
© 1981 Kingsway's Thankyou Music*

228

1. Restore, O Lord,
the honour of your name,
in works of sov'reign pow'r
come shake the earth again,
that all may see
and come with rev'rent fear
to the living God
whose kingdom shall outlast the years.

2. Restore, O Lord,
in all the earth your fame,
and in our time revive
the Church that bears your name.
And in your anger,
Lord, remember mercy,
O living God
whose mercy shall outlast the years.

229

*Rise and shine,
and give God his glory, glory.
Rise and shine,
and give God his glory, glory.
Rise and shine,
and give God his glory, glory,
children of the Lord.*

1. The Lord said to Noah:
'There's gonna be a floody, floody.'
Lord said to Noah:
'There's gonna be a floody, floody.
Get those children
out of the muddy, muddy,
children of the Lord.'

Continued overleaf

2. So Noah, he built him,
   he built him an arky, arky,
   Noah, he built him,
   he built him an arky, arky,
   built it out of
   hickory barky, barky,
   children of the Lord.

   Rise and shine,
   and give God his glory, glory.
   Rise and shine,
   and give God his glory, glory.
   Rise and shine,
   and give God his glory, glory,
   children of the Lord.

3. The animals, they came on,
   they came on, by twosies, twosies,
   animals, they came on,
   they came on, by twosies, twosies,
   elephants and
   kangaroosies, roosies,
   children of the Lord.

4. It rained and poured
   for forty daysies, daysies,
   rained and poured
   for forty daysies, daysies,
   nearly drove those
   animals crazyies, crazyies,
   children of the Lord.

5. The sun came out
   and dried up the landy, landy,
   sun came out
   and dried up the landy, landy,
   everything was
   fine and dandy, dandy,
   children of the Lord.

6. If you get to heaven
   before I do-sies, do-sies,
   you get to heaven
   before I do-sies, do-sies,
   tell those angels,
   I'm comin' too-sies, too-sies,
   children of the Lord.

Based on Genesis 6:4

230

1. See amid the winter's snow,
   born for us on earth below,
   see the tender Lamb appears,
   promised from eternal years.

   Hail, thou ever-blessèd morn,
   hail, redemption's happy dawn!
   Sing through all Jerusalem,
   Christ is born in Bethlehem.

2. Lo, within a manger lies
   he who built the starry skies;
   he who, throned in heights sublime,
   sits amid the cherubim.

3. Say, ye holy shepherds, say,
   what your joyful news today?
   Wherefore have ye left your sheep
   on the lonely mountain steep?

4. 'As we watched at dead of night,
   lo, we saw a wondrous light;
   angels, singing peace on earth,
   told us of the Saviour's birth.'

5. Sacred infant, all divine,
   what a tender love was thine,
   thus to come from highest bliss,
   down to such a world as this!

6. Virgin mother, Mary blest,
   by the joys that fill thy breast,
   pray for us, that we may prove
   worthy of the Saviour's love.

   Edward Caswall (1814-1878)

231

1. See him lying on a bed of straw:
   a draughty stable with an open door.
   Mary cradling the babe she bore:
   the Prince of Glory is his name.

   O now carry me to Bethlehem
   to see the Lord of love again:
   just as poor as was the stable then,
   the Prince of Glory when he came!

2. Star of silver, sweep across the skies,
   show where Jesus in the manger lies;
   shepherds, swiftly from your stupor
       rise
   to see the Saviour of the world!

3. Angels, sing again the song you sang,
   sing the glory of God's gracious plan;
   sing that Bethl'em's little baby can
   be the saviour of us all.

4. Mine are riches, from your poverty;
   from your innocence, eternity;
   mine, forgiveness by your death
       for me,
   child of sorrow for my joy.

   Michael Perry (b. 1942)

232

1. Seek ye first the kingdom of God,
   and his righteousness,
   and all these things shall be added
       unto you;
   allelu, alleluia.

Alleluia, alleluia, alleluia,
allelu, alleluia.

2. You shall not live by bread alone,
   but by ev'ry word
   that proceeds from the mouth of God;
   allelu, alleluia.

3. Ask and it shall be given unto you,
   seek and ye shall find;
   knock, and it shall be opened unto
       you;
   allelu, alleluia.

   v. 1: Karen Lafferty (b. 1948)
   vs. 2 & 3: unknown; based on Matthew 4:4, 6:33, 7:7
   © 1972 Maranatha! Music/CopyCare Ltd

233

1. Shall we not love thee, Mother dear,
   whom Jesus loves so well,
   and to his glory year by year
   thy praise and honour tell?

2. Thee did he choose from whom to take
   true flesh, his flesh to be;
   in it to suffer for our sake,
   and by it make us free.

3. O wondrous depth of love divine,
   that he should bend so low;
   and, Mary, O what joy was thine
   the Saviour's love to know.

4. Joy to be mother of the Lord,
   yet thine the truer bliss,
   in ev'ry thought and deed and word
   to be for ever his.

Continued overleaf

5. Now in the realm of life above
   close to thy Son thou art,
   while on thy soul glad streams of love
   flow from his sacred heart.

6. Jesu, the Virgin's holy Son,
   praise we thy mother blest;
   grant when our earthly course is run,
   life with the saints at rest.

Henry Williams Baker (1821-1877)

234

1. Silent night, holy night.
   All is calm, all is bright,
   round yon virgin mother and child;
   holy infant, so tender and mild,
   sleep in heavenly peace,
   sleep in heavenly peace.

2. Silent night, holy night.
   Shepherds quake at the sight,
   glories stream from heaven afar,
   heav'nly hosts sing alleluia:
   Christ, the Saviour is born,
   Christ, the Saviour is born.

3. Silent night, holy night.
   Son of God, love's pure light,
   radiant beams from thy holy face,
   with the dawn of redeeming grace:
   Jesus, Lord, at thy birth,
   Jesus, Lord, at thy birth.

Joseph Mohr (1792-1848)
trans. John Freeman Young (1820-1885)

235

1. Sing lullaby!
   Lullaby baby, now reclining,
   sing lullaby!
   Hush, do not wake the infant king.
   Angels are watching,
   stars are shining
   over the place where he is lying:
   sing lullaby!

2. Sing lullaby!
   Lullaby baby, now a-sleeping,
   sing lullaby!
   Hush, do not wake the infant king.
   Soon will come sorrow
   with the morning,
   soon will come bitter grief and
      weeping:
   sing lullaby!

3. Sing lullaby!
   Lullaby baby, now a-dozing,
   sing lullaby!
   Hush, do not wake the infant king.
   Soon comes the cross,
   the nails, the piercing,
   then in the grave at last reposing:
   sing lullaby!

4. Sing lullaby!
   Lullaby! is the babe awaking?
   Sing lullaby.
   Hush, do not stir the infant king.
   Dreaming of Easter,
   gladsome morning,
   conquering death, its bondage
      breaking:
   sing lullaby!

Sabine Baring-Gould (1834-1924)

236

1. Sing to God new songs of worship,
   all his deeds are marvellous;
   he has brought salvation to us
   with his hand and holy arm:
   he has shown to all the nations
   righteousness and saving pow'r;
   he recalled his truth and mercy
   to his people Israel.

2. Sing to God new songs of worship,
   earth has seen his victory;
   let the lands of earth be joyful
   praising him with thankfulness:
   sound upon the harp his praises,
   play to him with melody;
   let the trumpets sound his triumph,
   show your joy to God the king!

3. Sing to God new songs of worship,
   let the sea now make a noise;
   all on earth and in the waters
   sound your praises to the Lord:
   let the hills be joyful together,
   let the rivers clap their hands,
   for with righteousness and justice
   he will come to judge the earth.

   Michael Baughen (b. 1930) from Psalm 98

2. Sing we, too, of Mary's sorrows,
   of the sword that pierced her through,
   when beneath the cross of Jesus
   she his weight of suff'ring knew,
   looked upon her Son and Saviour
   reigning high on Calv'ry's tree,
   saw the price of our redemption
   paid to set the sinner free.

3. Sing again the joys of Mary
   when she saw the risen Lord,
   and, in prayer with Christ's apostles,
   waited on his promised word:
   from on high the blazing glory
   of the Spirit's presence came,
   heav'nly breath of God's own being,
   manifest through wind and flame.

4. Sing the greatest joy of Mary
   when on earth her work was done,
   and the Lord of all creation
   brought her to his heav'nly home:
   virgin mother, Mary blessèd,
   raised on high and crowned with
        grace,
   may your Son, the world's redeemer,
   grant us all to see his face.

   George Bourne Timms (b. 1910)

237

1. Sing we of the blessèd Mother
   who received the angel's word,
   and obedient to his summons
   bore in love the infant Lord;
   sing we of the joys of Mary
   at whose breast that child was fed
   who is Son of God eternal
   and the everlasting Bread.

238

1. Soul of my Saviour,
   sanctify my breast;
   Body of Christ,
   be thou my saving guest;
   Blood of my Saviour,
   bathe me in thy tide,
   wash me with water
   flowing from thy side.

   Continued overleaf

2. Strength and protection
   may thy passion be;
   O blessèd Jesus,
   hear and answer me;
   deep in thy wounds, Lord,
   hide and shelter me;
   so shall I never,
   never part from thee.

3. Guard and defend me
   from the foe malign;
   in death's dread moments
   make me only thine;
   call me, and bid me
   come to thee on high,
   where I may praise thee
   with thy saints for ay.

Ascribed to Pope John XXII (1249-1334)
trans. unknown

239

Spirit of the living God,
fall afresh on me.
Spirit of the living God,
fall afresh on me.
Melt me, mould me,
fill me, use me.
Spirit of the living God,
fall afresh on me.

Daniel Iverson (1890-1972)
© 1963 Birdwing Music/Alliance Media Ltd/CopyCare Ltd

240

Spirit of the living God,
fall afresh on me;
Spirit of the living God,
fall afresh on me;
fill me anew, fill me anew;
Spirit of the Lord,
fall afresh on me.

Paul Armstrong
© 1984 Restoration Music Ltd/Sovereign Music UK

241

1. Stand up, stand up for Jesus,
   stand up before his cross,
   an instrument of torture
   inflicting pain and loss;
   transformed by his obedience
   to God's redeeming plan,
   the cross was overpowered
   by Christ, both God and man.

2. Stand up, stand up for Jesus,
   be counted as his own;
   his gospel of forgiveness
   he cannot spread alone.
   The love which draws us to him,
   he calls us out to share;
   he calls us to the margins
   to be his presence there.

3. Stand up, stand up for Jesus,
   in faith and hope be strong,
   stand firm for right and justice,
   opposed to sin and wrong.
   Give comfort to the wounded,
   and care for those in pain,
   for Christ, in those who suffer,
   is crucified again.

4. Stand up, stand up for Jesus,
who reigns as King of kings,
be ready for the challenge
of faith his kingship brings.
He will not force obedience,
he gives to each the choice
to turn from all that's holy,
or in his love rejoice.

5. Stand up, stand up for Jesus,
give courage to the weak,
be unashamed to praise him,
be bold his name to speak.
Confront the cross unflinching,
Christ's love has set us free;
he conquered death for ever
and lives eternally.

Jean Holloway (b. 1939)

242

Stay with me,
remain here with me,
watching and praying,
watching and praying.

Taizé Community

243

*Steal away, steal away,
steal away to Jesus.
Steal away, steal away home,
I ain't got long to stay here.*

1. My Lord, he calls me,
he calls me by the thunder.
The trumpet sounds within my soul;
I ain't got long to stay here.

2. Green trees are bending,
the sinner stands a-trembling.
The trumpet sounds within my soul;
I ain't got long to stay here.

3. My Lord, he calls me,
he calls me by the lightning.
The trumpet sounds within my soul;
I ain't got long to stay here.

Spiritual

244

1. Such love, pure as the whitest snow;
such love weeps for the shame I know;
such love, paying the debt I owe;
O Jesus, such love.

2. Such love, stilling my restlessness;
such love, filling my emptiness;
such love, showing me holiness;
O Jesus, such love.

3. Such love springs from eternity;
such love, streaming through history;
such love, fountain of life to me;
O Jesus, such love.

Graham Kendrick (b. 1950)
© 1988 Make Way Music Ltd

245

1. Sweet sacrament divine,
hid in thy earthly home,
lo, round thy lowly shrine,
with suppliant hearts we come;
Jesus, to thee our voice we raise,
in songs of love and heartfelt praise,
sweet sacrament divine,
sweet sacrament divine.

Continued overleaf

2. Sweet sacrament of peace,
   dear home of ev'ry heart,
   where restless yearnings cease,
   and sorrows all depart;
   there in thine ear all trustfully
   we tell our tale of misery,
   sweet sacrament of peace,
   sweet sacrament of peace.

3. Sweet sacrament of rest,
   ark from the ocean's roar,
   within thy shelter blest
   soon may we reach the shore;
   save us, for still the tempest raves,
   save, lest we sink beneath the waves,
   sweet sacrament of rest,
   sweet sacrament of rest.

4. Sweet sacrament divine,
   earth's light and jubilee,
   in thy far depths doth shine
   thy Godhead's majesty;
   sweet light, so shine on us, we pray,
   that worthless joys may fade away,
   sweet sacrament divine,
   sweet sacrament divine.

   Francis Stanfield (1835-1914) alt.

246

1. Take my life, and let it be
   consecrated, Lord, to thee;
   take my moments and my days,
   let them flow in ceaseless praise.

2. Take my hands, and let them move
   at the impulse of thy love;
   take my feet, and let them be
   swift and beautiful for thee.

3. Take my voice, and let me sing
   always, only, for my King;
   take my lips, and let them be
   filled with messages from thee.

4. Take my silver and my gold;
   not a mite would I withhold;
   take my intellect, and use
   ev'ry pow'r as thou shalt choose.

5. Take my will, and make it thine:
   it shall be no longer mine;
   take my heart: it is thine own;
   it shall be thy royal throne.

6. Take my love; my Lord, I pour
   at thy feet its treasure-store;
   take myself, and I will be
   ever, only, all for thee.

   Frances Ridley Havergal (1836-1879)

247

1. Thank you, Lord, for this new day,
   thank you, Lord, for this new day,
   thank you, Lord, for this new day,
   right where we are.

   *Alleluia, praise the Lord,
   alleluia, praise the Lord,
   alleluia, praise the Lord,
   right where we are.*

2. Thank you, Lord, for food to eat,
   thank you, Lord, for food to eat,
   thank you, Lord, for food to eat,
   right where we are.

3. Thank you, Lord, for clothes to wear,
   thank you, Lord, for clothes to wear,
   thank you, Lord, for clothes to wear,
   right where we are.

4. Thank you, Lord, for all your gifts,
   thank you, Lord, for all your gifts,
   thank you, Lord, for all your gifts,
   right where we are.

   *Diane Davis Andrew,
   adapted by Geoffrey Marshall-Taylor*
   © 1971 Celebration/Kingsway's Thankyou Music

248

Thanks for the fellowship
found at this meal,
thanks for a day refreshed;
thanks to the Lord
for his presence we feel,
thanks for the food he blessed.
Joyfully sing praise to the Lord,
praise to the risen Son,
alleluia, ever adored,
pray that his will be done.
As he was known
in the breaking of bread,
now is he known again;
and by his hand
have the hungry been fed,
thanks be to Christ. Amen!

Jean Holloway (b. 1939)

249

1. The angel Gabriel
   from heaven came,
   his wings as drifted snow,
   his eyes as flame.
   'All hail', said he,
   'thou lowly maiden, Mary,
   most highly favoured lady.' Gloria!

2. 'For known a blessèd Mother
   thou shalt be.
   All generations laud
   and honour thee.
   Thy Son shall be Emmanuel,
   by seers foretold,
   most highly favoured lady.' Gloria!

3. Then gentle Mary meekly
   bowed her head.
   'To me be as it pleaseth God,'
   she said.
   'My soul shall laud and magnify
   his holy name.'
   Most highly favoured lady! Gloria!

4. Of her, Emmanuel,
   the Christ, was born
   in Bethlehem,
   all on a Christmas morn;
   and Christian folk throughout
   the world will ever say:
   'Most highly favoured lady.' Gloria!

Sabine Baring-Gould (1834-1924)

250

1. The first Nowell the angel did say
   was to certain poor shepherds in fields
   as they lay;
   in fields where they lay keeping their
   sheep,
   on a cold winter's night that was so
   deep.

   Nowell, Nowell, Nowell, Nowell,
   born is the King of Israel!

2. They lookèd up and saw a star,
   shining in the east, beyond them far,
   and to the earth it gave great light,
   and so it continued both day and night.

3. And by the light of that same star,
   three wise men came from country far;
   to seek for a king was their intent,
   and to follow the star wherever it went.

Continued overleaf

4. This star drew nigh to the north-west,
   o'er Bethlehem it took its rest,
   and there it did both stop and stay
   right over the place where Jesus lay.

   Nowell, Nowell, Nowell, Nowell,
   born is the King of Israel!

5. Then entered in those wise men three,
   full rev'rently upon their knee,
   and offered there in his presence,
   their gold and myrrh and frankincense.

6. Then let us all with one accord
   sing praises to our heav'nly Lord,
   that hath made heav'n and earth of
      naught,
   and with his blood mankind hath
      bought.

   from William Sandys' 'Christmas Carols,
   Ancient and Modern' (1833)

251

1. The holly and the ivy,
   when they are both full grown,
   of all the trees that are in the wood
   the holly bears the crown.

   The rising of the sun
   and the running of the deer,
   the playing of the merry organ,
   sweet singing in the choir.

2. The holly bears a blossom,
   white as the lily flow'r,
   and Mary bore sweet Jesus Christ
   to be our sweet Saviour.

3. The holly bears a berry,
   as red as any blood,
   and Mary bore sweet Jesus Christ
   to do poor sinners good.

4. The holly bears a prickle,
   as sharp as any thorn,
   and Mary bore sweet Jesus Christ
   on Christmas day in the morn.

5. The holly bears a bark,
   as bitter as any gall,
   and Mary bore sweet Jesus Christ
   for to redeem us all.

6. The holly and the ivy,
   when they are both full grown,
   of all the trees that are in the wood
   the holly bears the crown.

   Traditional

252

1. The ink is black, the page is white,
   together we learn to read and write,
   to read and write;
   and now a child can understand
   this is the law of all the land,
   all the land;
   the ink is black, the page is white,
   together we learn to read and write,
   to read and write.

2. The slate is black, the chalk is white,
   the words stand out so clear and bright,
   so clear and bright;
   and now at last we plainly see
   the alphabet of liberty,
   liberty;
   the slate is black, the chalk is white,
   together we learn to read and write,
   to read and write.

3. A child is black, a child is white,
the whole world looks upon the sight,
upon the sight;
for very well the whole world knows,
this is the way that freedom grows,
freedom grows;
a child is black, a child is white,
together we learn to read and write,
to read and write.

4. The world is black, the world is white,
it turns by day and then by night,
and then by night;
it turns so each and ev'ry one
can take his station in the sun,
in the sun;
the world is black, the world is white,
together we learn to read and write,
to read and write.

David Arkin

253

1. The King is among us,
his spirit is here,
let's draw near and worship,
let songs fill the air.

2. He looks down upon us,
delight in his face,
enjoying his children's love,
enthralled by our praise.

3. For each child is special,
accepted and loved,
a love gift from Jesus
to his Father above.

4. And now he is giving
his gifts to us all,
for no one is worthless
and each one is called.

5. The Spirit's anointing
on all flesh comes down,
and we shall be channels
for works like his own.

6. We come now believing
your promise of pow'r,
for we are your people
and this is your hour.

7. The King is among us,
his Spirit is here,
let's draw near and worship,
let songs fill the air.

Graham Kendrick (b. 1950)
© 1981 Kingsway's Thankyou Music

254

1. The Lord is King! lift up thy voice,
O earth, and all ye heav'ns, rejoice;
from world to world the joy shall ring:
'The Lord omnipotent is King!'

2. He reigns! ye saints, exalt your strains;
your God is King, your Saviour reigns;
and he is at the Father's side,
the Man of Love, the Crucified.

3. Alike pervaded by his eye
all parts of his dominion lie:
this world of ours and worlds unseen,
and thin the boundary between.

4. One Lord one empire all secures;
he reigns, and endless life is yours;
through earth and heav'n one song
    shall ring:
'The Lord omnipotent is King!'

Josiah Conder (1789-1855) alt.

255

The Lord is my light,
my light and salvation;
in God I trust,
in God I trust.

Based on Psalm 27

256

The Lord is my song,
the Lord is my praise:
all my hope comes from God.
The Lord is my song,
the Lord is my praise:
God, the well-spring of life.

Taizé Community

257

1. The Lord's my shepherd, I'll not want.
   He makes me down to lie
   in pastures green. He leadeth me
   the quiet waters by.
   He leadeth me, he leadeth me
   the quiet waters by.

2. My soul he doth restore again,
   and me to walk doth make
   within the paths of righteousness,
   e'en for his own name's sake.
   within the paths of righteousness,
   e'en for his own name's sake.

3. Yea, though I walk in death's dark vale,
   yet will I fear none ill.
   For thou art with me, and thy rod
   and staff me comfort still.
   For thou art with me, and thy rod
   and staff me comfort still.

4. My table thou hast furnishèd
   in presence of my foes:
   my head thou dost with oil anoint,
   and my cup overflows.
   my head thou dost with oil anoint,
   and my cup overflows.

5. Goodness and mercy all my life
   shall surely follow me.
   And in God's house for evermore
   my dwelling-place shall be.
   And in God's house for evermore
   my dwelling-place shall be.

Psalm 23 from 'The Scottish Psalter' (1650)

258

1. The Spirit lives to set us free,
   walk, walk in the light.
   He binds us all in unity,
   walk, walk in the light.

   Walk in the light,
   walk in the light,
   walk in the light,
   walk in the light of the Lord.

2. Jesus promised life to all,
   walk, walk in the light.
   The dead were wakened by his call,
   walk, walk in the light.

3. He died in pain on Calvary,
   walk, walk in the light,
   to save the lost like you and me,
   walk, walk in the light.

4. We know his death was not the end,
   walk, walk in the light.
   He gave his Spirit to be our friend,
   walk, walk in the light.

5. By Jesus' love our wounds are healed,
walk, walk in the light.
The Father's kindness is revealed,
walk, walk in the light.

6. The Spirit lives in you and me,
walk, walk in the light.
His light will shine for all to see,
walk, walk in the light.

Damian Lundy (b. 1944)

259

1. The Virgin Mary
had a baby boy,
the Virgin Mary
had a baby boy,
the Virgin Mary
had a baby boy,
and they said that his
name was Jesus.

He came from the glory,
he came from the glorious kingdom.
He came from the glory,
he came from the glorious kingdom.
O yes, believer.
O yes, believer.
He came from the glory,
he came from the glorious kingdom.

2. The angels sang
when the baby was born, (3)
and proclaimed him
the Saviour Jesus.

3. The wise men saw
where the baby was born, (3)
and they saw that his
name was Jesus.

Traditional West Indian

260

1. There are hundreds of sparrows,
thousands, millions,
they're two a penny,
far too many there must be;
there are hundreds and thousands,
millions of sparrows,
but God knows ev'ry one
and God knows me.

2. There are hundreds of flowers,
thousands, millions,
and flowers fair
the meadows wear for all to see;
there are hundreds and thousands,
millions of flowers,
but God knows ev'ry one
and God knows me.

3. There are hundreds of planets,
thousands, millions,
way out in space
each has a place by God's decree;
there are hundreds and thousands,
millions of planets,
but God knows ev'ry one
and God knows me.

4. There are hundreds of children,
thousands, millions,
and yet their names
are written on God's memory,
there are hundreds and thousands,
millions of children,
but God knows ev'ry one
and God knows me.

John Gowans

261

1. There is a Redeemer,
   Jesus, God's own Son,
   precious Lamb of God, Messiah,
   Holy One.

   Thank you, O my Father,
   for giving us your Son,
   and leaving your Spirit
   till the work on earth is done.

2. Jesus, my Redeemer,
   name above all names,
   precious Lamb of God, Messiah,
   O for sinners slain.

3. When I stand in glory,
   I will see his face,
   and there I'll serve my King for ever,
   in that holy place.

   Melody Green, based on Scripture
   © Birdwing Music/BMG Songs Inc/
   Alliance Media Ltd/CopyCare Ltd

262

1. There's a wideness in God's mercy,
   like the wideness of the sea;
   there's a kindness in his justice,
   which is more than liberty.
   There is no place where earth's sorrows
   are more felt than up in heav'n;
   there is no place where earth's failings
   have such kindly judgement giv'n.

2. But we make his love too narrow
   by false limits of our own;
   and we magnify his strictness
   with a zeal he will not own.
   There is plentiful redemption
   in the blood that has been shed,
   there is joy for all the members
   in the sorrows of the Head.

3. For the love of God is broader
   than the scope of human mind,
   and the heart of the Eternal
   is most wonderfully kind.
   If our love were but more simple,
   we should take him at his word;
   and our hearts would find assurance
   in the promise of the Lord.

   Frederick William Faber (1814-1863) alt.

263

1. Think of a world
   without any flowers,
   think of a world
   without any trees,
   think of a sky
   without any sunshine,
   think of the air
   without any breeze.
   We thank you, Lord,
   for flow'rs and trees and sunshine,
   we thank you, Lord,
   and praise your holy name.

2. Think of a world
   without any animals,
   think of a field
   without any herd,
   think of a stream
   without any fishes,
   think of a dawn
   without any bird.
   We thank you, Lord,
   for all your living creatures,
   we thank you, Lord,
   and praise your holy name.

3. Think of a world
   without any people,
   think of a street
   with no-one living there,
   think of a town
   without any houses,
   no-one to love
   and nobody to care.
   We thank you, Lord,
   for families and friendships,
   we thank you, Lord,
   and praise your holy name.

   Doreen Newport (b. 1927)

264

1. This is my body, broken for you,
   bringing you wholeness, making you
   free.
   Take it and eat it, and when you do,
   do it in love for me.

2. This is my blood, poured out for you,
   bringing forgiveness, making you free.
   Take it and drink it, and when you do,
   do it in love for me.

3. Back to my Father soon I shall go.
   Do not forget me; then you will see
   I am still with you, and you will know
   you're very close to me.

4. Filled with my Spirit, how you will
   grow!
   You are my branches; I am the tree.
   If you are faithful, others will know
   you are alive in me.

5. Love one another: I have loved you,
   and I have shown you how to be free;
   serve one another, and when you do,
   do it in love for me.

   vs. 1 & 2: Jimmy Owens,
   vs. 3-5: Damian Lundy (b. 1944)
   © 1978 Bud John Songs/Alliance Media Ltd/CopyCare Ltd

265

1. This is my will, my one command,
   that love should dwell among you all.
   This is my will, that you should love
   as I have shown that I love you.

2. No greater love can be than this:
   to choose to die to save one's friends.
   You are my friends if you obey
   what I command that you should do.

3. I call you now no longer slaves;
   no slave knows all his master does.
   I call you friends, for all I hear
   my Father say you hear from me.

4. You chose not me, but I chose you,
   that you should go and bear much
   fruit.
   I chose you out that you in me
   should bear much fruit that will abide.

5. All that you ask my Father dear
   for my name's sake you shall receive.
   This is my will, my one command,
   that love should dwell in each, in all.

   James Quinn (b. 1919)

266

1. This is the day, this is the day
   that the Lord has made,
   that the Lord has made;
   we will rejoice, we will rejoice
   and glad in it, and be glad in it.
   This is the day that the Lord has made;
   we will rejoice and be glad in it.
   This is the day, this is the day
   that the Lord has made.

2. This is the day, this is the day
   when he rose again,
   when he rose again;
   we will rejoice, we will rejoice
   and be glad in it, and be glad in it.
   This is the day when he rose again;
   we will rejoice and be glad in it.
   This is the day, this is the day
   when he rose again.

3. This is the day, this is the day
   when the Spirit came,
   when the Spirit came;
   we will rejoice, we will rejoice
   and be glad in it, and be glad in it.
   This is the day when the Spirit came;
   we will rejoice and be glad in it.
   This is the day, this is the day
   when the Spirit came.

   Les Garrett (b. 1944) based on Psalm 118
   © 1967 Scripture in Song/Integrity's Hosanna! Music

267

1. This joyful Eastertide,
   away with sin and sorrow,
   my love, the Crucified,
   hath sprung to life this morrow.

Had Christ, that once was slain,
ne'er burst his three-day prison,
our faith had been in vain:
but now hath Christ arisen,
arisen, arisen, arisen.

2. My flesh in hope shall rest,
   and for a season slumber:
   till trump from east to west
   shall wake the dead in number.

3. Death's flood hath lost its chill,
   since Jesus crossed the river:
   lover of souls, from ill
   my passing soul deliver.

   George Ratcliffe Woodward (1848-1934)

268

This little light of mine,
I'm gonna let it shine.
This little light of mine,
I'm gonna let it shine.
This little light of mine,
I'm gonna let it shine,
let it shine, let it shine,
let it shine.

1. The light that shines
   is the light of love,
   lights the darkness
   from above,
   it shines on me
   and it shines on you,
   and shows what the
   power of love can do.
   I'm gonna shine my light
   both far and near,
   I'm gonna shine my light
   both bright and clear.
   Where there's a dark
   corner in this land,
   I'm gonna let my
   little light shine.

2. On Monday he gave
   me the gift of love.
   Tuesday peace came
   from above.
   On Wednesday he told me
   to have more faith.
   On Thursday he gave me
   a little more grace.
   Friday he told me
   just to watch and pray.
   Saturday he told me
   just what to say.
   On Sunday he gave me
   the pow'r divine to let
   my little light shine.

   Traditional

269

*This world you have made
is a beautiful place;
it tells the pow'r of your love.
We rejoice in the beauty
of your world,
from the seas
to the heavens above.*

1. The morning whispers of purity;
   the evening of your peace;
   the thunder booms your exuberance
   in the awesome pow'r you release.

2. The tenderness of a new-born child;
   the gentleness of the rain;
   simplicity in a single cell;
   and complexity in a brain.

3. Your stillness rests in a silent pool;
   infinity drifts in space;
   your grandeur straddles the mountain
      tops;
   and we see your face in each face.

   Susan Sayers (b. 1946)

270

1. Thy way, not mine, O Lord,
   however dark it be;
   lead me by thine own hand,
   choose out the path for me.

2. Smooth let it be or rough,
   it will be still the best;
   winding or straight, it leads
   right onward to thy rest.

3. I dare not choose my lot;
   I would not if I might:
   choose thou for me, my God,
   so shall I walk aright.

4. The kingdom that I seek
   is thine, so let the way
   that leads to it be thine,
   else I must surely stray.

5. Take thou my cup, and it
   with joy or sorrow fill,
   as best to thee may seem;
   choose thou my good and ill.

6. Choose thou for me my friends,
   my sickness or my health;
   choose thou my cares for me,
   my poverty or wealth.

7. Not mine, not mine, the choice
   in things or great or small;
   be thou my guide, my strength,
   my wisdom, and my all.

   Horatius Bonar (1808-1889)

271

1. To God be the glory!
   great things he hath done;
   so loved he the world
   that he gave us his Son;
   who yielded his life
   an atonement for sin,
   and opened the life-gate
   that all may go in.

   Praise the Lord, praise the Lord!
   let the earth hear his voice;
   praise the Lord, praise the Lord!
   let the people rejoice:
   O come to the Father,
   through Jesus the Son,
   and give him the glory;
   great things he hath done.

2. O perfect redemption,
   the purchase of blood!
   to ev'ry believer
   the promise of God;
   the vilest offender
   who truly believes,
   that moment from Jesus
   a pardon receives.

3. Great things he hath taught us,
   great things he hath done,
   and great our rejoicing
   through Jesus the Son;
   but purer, and higher,
   and greater will be
   our wonder, our rapture,
   when Jesus we see.

   Frances Jane van Alstyne
   (Fanny J. Crosby) (1820-1915)

272

Ubi caritas et amor.
Ubi caritas Deus ibi est.

1. Your love, O Jesus Christ,
   has gathered us together.

2. May your love, O Jesus Christ,
   be foremost in our lives.

3. Let us love one another
   as God has loved us.

4. Let us be one in love together
   in the one bread of Christ.

5. The love of God in Jesus Christ
   bears eternal joy.

6. The love of God in Jesus Christ
   will never have a   d.

   Taizé Community

273

1. Unto us a boy is born!
   King of all creation;
   came he to a world forlorn,
   the Lord of ev'ry nation,
   the Lord of ev'ry nation.

2. Cradled in a stall was he,
   watched by cows and asses;
   but the very beasts could see
   that he the world surpasses,
   that he the world surpasses.

3. Then the fearful Herod cried,
   'Pow'r is mine in Jewry!'
   So the blameless children died
   the victims of his fury,
   the victims of his fury.

4. Now may Mary's Son, who came
long ago to love us,
lead us all with hearts aflame
unto the joys above us,
unto the joys above us.

5. Omega and Alpha he!
Let the organ thunder,
while the choir with peals of glee
shall rend the air asunder,
shall rend the air asunder.

15th century trans. Percy Dearmer (1867-1936) alt.

274

*Wait for the Lord, whose day is near.
Wait for the Lord: keep watch, take
heart!*

1. Prepare the way for the Lord.
Make a straight path for him.

2. The glory of the Lord
shall be revealed.

3. All the earth will see the Lord.

4. Rejoice in the Lord always:
he is at hand.

5. Seek first the kingdom of God,
seek and you shall find.

6. Joy and gladness for all
who seek the Lord.

7. I waited for the Lord:
he heard my cry.

8. Our eyes are fixed
on the Lord our God.

9. O Lord, show us your way.
Guide us in your truth.

10. Prepare the way of the Lord.

Taizé Community, based on Scripture

275

1. Wake, O wake! with tidings thrilling
the watchmen all
the air are filling:
arise, Jerusalem, arise!
Midnight strikes! no more delaying,
'The hour has come!'
we hear them saying.
Where are ye all, ye maidens wise?
The Bridegroom comes in sight,
raise high your torches bright!
Alleluia!
The wedding song
swells loud and strong:
go forth and join the festal throng.

2. Sion hears the watchmen shouting,
her heart leaps up
with joy undoubting,
she stands and waits with eager eyes;
see her Friend from heav'n descending,
adorned with truth
and grace unending!
her light burns clear, her star doth rise.
Now come, thou precious Crown,
Lord Jesu, God's own son!
Hosanna!
Let us prepare
to follow there,
where in thy supper we may share.

Continued overleaf

3. Ev'ry soul in thee rejoices;
   from earthly and
   angelic voices
   be glory giv'n to thee alone!
   Now the gates of pearl receive us,
   thy presence never more
   shall leave us,
   we stand with angels round thy throne.
   Earth cannot give below
   the bliss thou dost bestow.
   Alleluia!
   Grant us to raise,
   to length of days,
   the triumph-chorus of thy praise.

   Philipp Nicolai (1556-1608)
   trans. Francis Crawford Burkitt (1864-1935) alt.

276

1. We believe in God the Father,
   maker of the universe,
   and in Christ his Son our Saviour,
   come to us by virgin birth.
   We believe he died to save us,
   bore our sins, was crucified;
   then from death he rose victorious,
   ascended to the Father's side.

   Jesus, Lord of all, Lord of all; (4)
   name above all names,
   name above all names!

2. We believe he sends his Spirit
   on his Church with gifts of pow'r;
   God, his word of truth affirming,
   sends us to the nations now.
   He will come again in glory,
   judge the living and the dead:
   ev'ry knee shall bow before him,
   then must ev'ry tongue confess.

   Graham Kendrick (b. 1950)
   © 1986 Kingsway's Thankyou Music

277

1. We three kings of Orient are;
   bearing gifts we traverse afar;
   field and fountain, moor and
      mountain,
   following yonder star.

   O star of wonder, star of night,
   star with royal beauty bright,
   westward leading, still proceeding,
   guide us to thy perfect light.

2. Born a King on Bethlehem plain,
   gold I bring, to crown him again,
   King for ever, ceasing never,
   over us all to reign.

3. Frankincense to offer have I,
   incense owns a Deity nigh,
   prayer and praising, gladly raising,
   worship him, God most high.

4. Myrrh is mine, its bitter perfume
   breathes a life of gathering gloom;
   sorrowing, sighing, bleeding, dying,
   sealed in the stone-cold tomb.

5. Glorious now behold him arise,
   King and God and sacrifice;
   alleluia, alleluia,
   earth to heav'n replies.

   John Henry Hopkins (1820-1891) alt.

278

1. We will lay our burden down,
   we will lay our burden down,
   we will lay our burden down
   in the hands of the risen Lord.

2. We will light the flame of love,
   we will light the flame of love,
   we will light the flame of love,
   as the hands of the risen Lord.

3. We will show both hurt and hope,
   we will show both hurt and hope,
   we will show both hurt and hope,
   like the hands of the risen Lord.

4. We will walk the path of peace,
   we will walk the path of peace,
   we will walk the path of peace,
   hand in hand with the risen Lord.

John L. Bell (b. 1949) and Graham Maule (b. 1958)

279

1. We'll walk the land with hearts on fire;
   and ev'ry step will be a prayer.
   Hope is rising, new day dawning;
   sound of singing fills the air.

2. Two thousand years, and still the flame
   is burning bright across the land.
   Hearts are waiting, longing, aching,
   for awakening once again.

   Let the flame burn brighter
   in the heart of the darkness,
   turning night to glorious day.
   Let the song grow louder,
   as our love grows stronger;
   let it shine!

3. We'll walk for truth, speak out for love;
   in Jesus' name we shall be strong,
   to lift the fallen, to save the children,
   to fill the nation with your song.

Graham Kendrick (b. 1950)
© 1989 Make Way Music Ltd

280

1. What a friend we have in Jesus,
   all our sins and griefs to bear!
   What a privilege to carry
   ev'rything to him in prayer!
   O what peace we often forfeit,
   O what needless pain we bear,
   all because we do not carry
   ev'rything to God in prayer!

2. Have we trials and temptations?
   Is there trouble anywhere?
   We should never be discouraged:
   take it to the Lord in prayer!
   Can we find a friend so faithful,
   who will all our sorrows share?
   Jesus knows our ev'ry weakness –
   take it to the Lord in prayer!

3. Are we weak and heavy-laden,
   cumbered with a load of care?
   Jesus only is our refuge,
   take it to the Lord in prayer!
   Do thy friends despise, forsake thee?
   Take it to the Lord in prayer!
   In his arms he'll take and shield thee,
   thou wilt find a solace there.

Joseph Medlicott Scriven (1819-1886)

281

1. What child is this who, laid to rest,
   on Mary's lap is sleeping?
   Whom angels greet
   with anthems sweet,
   while shepherds watch are keeping?
   This, this is Christ the King,
   whom shepherds guard and angels
     sing:
   come, greet the infant Lord,
   the babe, the Son of Mary!

Continued overleaf

2. Why lies he in such mean estate,
where ox and ass are feeding?
Good Christians, fear:
for sinners here
the silent Word is pleading.
Nails, spear, shall pierce him through,
the cross be borne for me, for you:
hail, hail the Word made flesh,
the babe, the Son of Mary!

3. So bring him incense, gold and myrrh,
come rich and poor, to own him.
The King of kings
salvation brings,
let loving hearts enthrone him.
Raise, raise the song on high,
the Virgin sings her lullaby:
joy, joy for Christ is born,
the babe, the Son of Mary!

William Chatterton Dix (1837-1898) alt.

282

1. When God Almighty came to earth,
he took the pain of Jesus' birth,
he took the flight of refugee,
and whispered: 'Humbly follow me.'

2. When God Almighty went to work,
carpenter's sweat he didn't shirk,
profit and loss he didn't flee,
and whispered: 'Humbly follow me.'

3. When God Almighty walked the street,
the critic's curse he had to meet,
the cynic's smile he had to see,
and whispered: 'Humbly follow me.'

4. When God Almighty met his folk,
of peace and truth he boldly spoke
to set the slave and tyrant free,
and whispered: 'Humbly follow me.'

5. When God Almighty took his place
to save the sometimes human race,
he took it boldly on a tree,
and whispered: 'Humbly follow me.'

6. When God Almighty comes again,
he'll meet us incognito as then;
and though no words may voice his plea,
he'll whisper: 'Are you following me?'

John L. Bell (b. 1949) and Graham Maule (b. 1958)

283

When I feel the touch
of your hand upon my life,
it causes me to sing a song,
that I love you, Lord.
So from deep within
my spirit singeth unto you,
you are my King, you are my God,
and I love you, Lord.

Keri Jones and David Matthew

284

When I look into your holiness,
when I gaze into your loveliness,
when all things that surround
become shadows in the light of you.
When I've found the joy
of reaching your heart,
when my will becomes
enthrall'd in your love,
when all things that surround
become shadows in the light of you:
I worship you, I worship you,
the reason I live is to worship you.
I worship you, I worship you,
the reason I live is to worship you.

Wayne and Cathy Perrin

285

1. When I needed a neighbour,
   were you there, were you there?
   When I needed a neighbour,
   were you there?

   And the creed and the colour
   and the name won't matter,
   were you there?

2. I was hungry and thirsty,
   were you there, were you there?
   I was hungry and thirsty,
   were you there?

3. I was cold, I was naked,
   were you there, were you there?
   I was cold, I was naked,
   were you there?

4. When I needed a shelter,
   were you there, were you there?
   When I needed a shelter,
   were you there?

5. When I needed a healer,
   were you there, were you there?
   When I needed a healer,
   were you there?

6. Wherever you travel,
   I'll be there, I'll be there,
   wherever you travel,
   I'll be there.

   Sydney Carter (b. 1915)

286

1. When, in our music,
   God is glorified,
   and adoration leaves
   no room for pride,
   it is as though
   the whole creation cried:
   Alleluia.

2. How often, making music,
   we have found
   a new dimension
   in the world of sound,
   as worship moved us
   to a more profound
   Alleluia!

3. So has the Church,
   in liturgy and song,
   in faith and love,
   through centuries of wrong,
   borne witness to the truth
   in ev'ry tongue:
   Alleluia!

4. And did not Jesus sing
   a psalm that night
   when utmost evil strove
   against the Light?
   Then let us sing,
   for whom he won the fight:
   Alleluia!

5. Let ev'ry instrument
   be tuned for praise!
   Let all rejoice
   who have a voice to raise!
   And may God give us
   faith to sing always:
   Alleluia!

   Fred Pratt Green (b. 1903)

287

1. When our God came to earth,
   not for him noble birth:
   he affirmed human worth
   from a humble manger,
   just another stranger.

   Let the poor rejoice!
   Let the mute give voice!
   Love is shown,
   God is known,
   Christ is born of Mary.

2. Not for kings was the word
   which the poor shepherds heard:
   hope renewed, grace conferred,
   and the hillside ringing
   with the angels' singing.

3. Bethlehem, humble town
   where the babe wears the crown,
   turns the world upside down:
   God so unexpected,
   homeless and rejected.

4. Let us sing Mary's song,
   bringing hope, righting wrong,
   heard with fear by the strong,
   poor and humble raising,
   God of justice praising.

   Michael Forster (b. 1946)

288

1. When we walk with the Lord
   in the light of his word,
   what a glory he sheds on our way!
   While we do his good will,
   he abides with us still,
   and with all who will trust and obey.

   Trust and obey, for there's no other way
   to be happy in Jesus, but to trust and obey.

2. Not a burden we bear,
   not a sorrow we share,
   but our toil he doth richly repay;
   not a grief nor a loss,
   not a frown nor a cross,
   but is blest if we trust and obey.

3. But we never can prove
   the delights of his love
   until all on the altar we lay;
   for the favour he shows,
   and the joy he bestows,
   are for them who will trust and obey.

4. Then in fellowship sweet
   we will sit at his feet,
   or we'll walk by his side in the way.
   What he says he will do,
   where he sends we will go,
   never fear, only trust and obey.

   John Henry Sammis (1846-1919)

289

1. Who is this so weak and helpless,
   child of lowly Hebrew maid,
   rudely in a stable sheltered,
   coldly in a manger laid?
   'Tis the Lord of all creation,
   who this wondrous path hath trod;
   he is God from everlasting,
   and to everlasting God.

2. Who is this – a Man of Sorrows,
   walking sadly life's hard way;
   homeless, weary, sighing, weeping
   over sin and Satan's sway?
   'Tis our God, our glorious Saviour,
   who beyond our mortal sight
   now for us a place prepareth
   free from grief and full of light.

3. Who is this – behold him raining
drops of blood upon the ground?
Who is this – despised, rejected,
mocked, insulted, beaten, bound?
'Tis our God, who gifts and graces
on his Church now poureth down;
all his faithful ones empow'ring
to partake in cross and crown.

4. Who is this that hangeth dying,
with the thieves on either side?
Nails his hands and feet are tearing,
and the spear hath pierced his side.
'Tis the God who ever liveth
'mid the shining ones on high,
in the glorious golden city
reigning everlastingly.

William Walsham How (1823-1897) alt.

290

1. Who put the colours in the rainbow?
Who put the salt into the sea?
Who put the cold into the snowflake?
Who made you and me?
Who put the hump upon the camel?
Who put the neck on the giraffe?
Who put the tail upon the monkey?
Who made hyenas laugh?
Who made whales and snails and
    quails?
Who made hogs and dogs and frogs?
Who made bats and rats and cats?
Who made ev'rything?

2. Who put the gold into the sunshine?
Who put the sparkle in the stars?
Who put the silver in the moonlight?
Who made Earth and Mars?
Who put the scent into the roses?
Who taught the honey bee to dance?

Who put the tree inside the acorn?
It surely can't be chance!
Who made seas and leaves and trees?
Who made snow and winds that blow?
Who made streams and rivers flow?
God made all of these!

Paul Booth

291

Wide, wide as the ocean,
high as the heavens above;
deep, deep as the deepest sea
is my Saviour's love.
I, though so unworthy,
still am a child of his care,
for his word teaches me that
his love reaches me ev'rywhere.

C. Austin Miles

292

1. Will you come and follow me
if I but call your name?
Will you go where you don't know,
and never be the same?
Will you let my love be shown,
will you let my name be known,
will you let my life be grown
in you, and you in me?

2. Will you leave yourself behind
if I but call your name?
Will you care for cruel and kind,
and never be the same?
Will you risk the hostile stare
should your life attract or scare,
will you let me answer prayer
in you, and you in me?

Continued overleaf

3. Will you let the blinded see
   if I but call your name?
   Will you set the pris'ners free,
   and never be the same?
   Will you kiss the leper clean
   and do such as this unseen,
   and admit to what I mean
   in you, and you in me?

4. Will you love the 'you' you hide
   if I but call your name?
   Will you quell the fear inside,
   and never be the same?
   Will you use the faith you've found
   to reshape the world around
   through my sight and touch and sound
   in you, and you in me?

5. Lord, your summons echoes true
   when you but call my name.
   Let me turn and follow you,
   and never be the same.
   In your company I'll go
   where your love and footsteps show.
   Thus I'll move and live and grow
   in you, and you in me.

John L. Bell (b. 1949) and Graham Maule (b. 1958)

293

1. Will your anchor hold
   in the storms of life,
   when the clouds unfold
   their wings of strife?
   When the strong tides lift,
   and the cables strain,
   will your anchor drift,
   or firm remain?

*We have an anchor
that keeps the soul
steadfast and sure
while the billows roll;
fastened to the rock
which cannot move,
grounded firm and deep
in the Saviour's love!*

2. Will your anchor hold
   in the straits of fear,
   when the breakers roar
   and the reef is near?
   While the surges rage,
   and the wild winds blow,
   shall the angry waves
   then your bark o'erflow?

3. Will your anchor hold
   in the floods of death,
   when the waters cold
   chill your latest breath?
   On the rising tide
   you can never fail,
   while your anchor holds
   within the veil.

4. Will your eyes behold
   through the morning light,
   the city of gold
   and the harbour bright?
   Will you anchor safe
   by the heav'nly shore,
   when life's storms are past
   for evermore?

Priscilla Jane Owens (1829-1899)

294

Within our darkest night,
you kindle the fire
that never dies away,
that never dies away.
Within our darkest night,
you kindle the fire
that never dies away,
that never dies away.

Taizé Community

295

You are beautiful
beyond description,
too marvellous for words,
too wonderful for comprehension
like nothing ever seen or heard.
Who can grasp your infinite wisdom?
Who can fathom
the depth of your love?
You are beautiful
beyond description,
Majesty enthroned above.
And I stand,
I stand in awe of you;
I stand, I stand in awe of you.
Holy God,
to whom all praise is due,
I stand in awe of you.

Mark Altrogge
© 1987 People of Destiny Int./Word Music Inc./
Word Music (UK)/CopyCare Ltd

296

You are the King of Glory,
you are the Prince of Peace,
you are the Lord of heav'n and earth,
you're the Son of righteousness.
Angels bow down before you,
worship and adore,
for you have the words
of eternal life,
you are Jesus Christ the Lord.
Hosanna to the Son of David!
Hosanna to the King of kings!
Glory in the highest heaven,
for Jesus the Messiah reigns!

Mavis Ford
© 1978 Springtide/Word Music (UK)/CopyCare Ltd

297

You shall go out with joy
and be led forth with peace,
and the mountains and the hills
shall break forth before you.
There'll be shouts of joy
and the trees of the field
shall clap,
shall clap their hands.
And the trees of the field
shall clap their hands,
and the trees of the field
shall clap their hands,
and the trees of the field
shall clap their hands,
and you'll go out with joy.

Stuart Dauermann (b. 1944) based on Isaiah 55:12
© 1975 Lillenas Publishing Co/Kingsway's Thankyou Music

Authors, Translators and Sources of Words

Scriptural Index

Index of Uses

Index of First Lines

Acknowledgements

The publishers wish to express their gratitude to the following for permission to use copyright material in this book:

The Executors of L.T.J. Arlott, 11 Victoria Street, Alderney, Channel Islands GY9 3AN for *God whose farm is all creation*.

Ateliers et Presses de Taizé, F-71250, Taizé-Communauté, France for *Adoramus te, Domine, Bless the Lord, Gloria, In the Lord I'll be ever thankful, Jesus, remember me, Kyrie, Laudate Dominum, Nada te turbe, O Lord, hear my prayer, Stay with me, The Lord is my light, The Lord is my song, Ubi caritas, Wait for the Lord* and *Within our darkest night*.

Mr Paul Booth for *Who put the colours in the rainbow?*

The Canterbury Press, St Mary's Works, St Mary's Plain, Norwich, Norfolk NR3 3BH for *Lift high the cross* © Hymns Ancient & Modern Ltd.

Cassell Plc, Wellington House, 125 Strand, London WC2R 0BB for *Forth in the peace of Christ we go* © Geoffrey Chapman and *This is my will* © Geoffrey Chapman. Also for *God is love* © Copyright revived 1996 Mowbray.

CopyCare Ltd, PO Box 77, Hailsham, East Sussex BN27 3EF for *Allelluia* (Donald Fishel) © 1973 Word of God Music/The Copyright Company, *As we are gathered* © 1979 Springtide/Word Music (UK), *Father, we adore you* © 1972 Maranatha! Music, *Father, we love you* © 1976 Maranatha! Music, *God forgave my sin* © 1972 Bud John Songs/Alliance Media Ltd, *Great is the Lord and most worthy of praise* © 1985 Body Songs, *He is exalted* © 1985 Straightway Music/Alliance Media Ltd, *Holy, holy, holy* © Bud John Songs/Alliance Media Ltd, *I love you, Lord* © 1978 Maranatha! Music, *I will enter his gates* © 1976 Maranatha! Music, *Jesus is Lord* © 1982 Springtide/Word Music (UK), *On a hill far away* © The Rodeheaver Co/Word Music Inc/Word Music (UK), *Open our eyes, Lord* © 1976 Maranatha! Music, *Spirit of the living God* © 1963 Birdwing Music/Alliance Media Ltd, *This is my body* © 1978 Bud John Songs/Alliance Media Ltd, *When I feel the touch* © 1978 Springtide/Word Music (UK), *Wide, wide as the ocean* © The Rodeheaver Co/Word Music Inc/Word Music (UK), *Hosanna to the Son of David* © 1978 Springtide/Word Music (UK), *I stand in awe* © 1987 People of Destiny Int/Word Music Inc/Word Music (UK), *Seek ye first* © 1972 Maranatha! Music, *I will sing the wondrous story* © Harper Collins Religious, and *There is a Redeemer* © 1982 Birdwing Music/BMG Songs Inc/Alliance Media Ltd.

Mrs M. Cross for *Father, Lord of all creation*.

J. Curwen & Son, 8/9 Frith Street, London W1V 5TZ for *All creatures of our God and King*. Also, *In our day of thanksgiving* © copyright revived 1996.

Dr. E.F. Downs for *God of grace and God of glory*.

The Rt. Rev'd. Timothy Dudley-Smith, 9 Ashlands, Ford, Salisbury, Wilts SP4 6DY for *Fill your hearts with joy, Jesus, Prince and Saviour* and *Lord, for the years*.

Durham Music Ltd, 1a Farm Place, London W8 7SX for *The Ink is Black* © 1970 Templeton Publishing Co Inc.

GIA Publications Inc, 7404 S. Mason Avenue, Chicago, IL 60638, USA for *I am the bread of life* © 1963 GIA Publications Inc. All rights reserved.

The Rev'd. M.J. Hancock for *Filled with the Spirit's power*.

David Higham Associates Ltd, 5-8 Lower John Street, Golden Square, London W1R 4HA for *Morning has broken* from 'The Children's Bells', published by Oxford University Press.

Hope Publishing Co, 380 South Main Place, Carol Stream, IL 60188, USA for *Great is thy faithfulness* © 1923 renewal 1951 Hope Publishing Co, and *New songs of celebration render* © 1974 Hope Publishing Co. All rights reserved. Used by permission.

Integrity Music Europe Ltd, Berkeley House, 26 Gildredge Road, Eastbourne, East Sussex BN21 4SA for *Hosanna* © 1985 Mercy/Vineyard Publishing, *I believe in Jesus* © 1985 Mercy/Vineyard Publishing, *I give you all the honour* © 1992 Mercy/Vineyard Publishing, *Holy and anointed one* © 1988 Mercy/Vineyard Publishing, *O let the Son of God* © 1979 Mercy/Vineyard Publishing and *Purify my heart* © 1985 Mercy/Vineyard Publishing, all administered in the UK and Eire by Integrity's Hosanna! Music. All rights reserved. International Copyright secured. Used by permission. Also for *Brother, let me be your servant* © 1977 Scripture in Song, *Jesus name above all names* © 1974 Scripture in Song and *This is the day* © 1967 Scripture in Song (A division of Integrity's Hosanna! Music). All rights reserved. International copyright secured. Used by permission.

The Iona Community, Community House, Pearce Institute, Govan, Glasgow G51 3UU for *Among us and before us, Bread is blessed and broken, Christ's is the world*, and *We will lay our burden down*, all © 1989 WGRG from the 'Love from below' collection; *Cloth for the cradle, Dance and sing, Heaven shall not wait, Inspired by love and anger, James and Andrew, Peter and John, When God almighty came to earth* and *Will you come and follow me*, all © 1987 WGRG from the 'Heaven shall not wait' collection and *Jesus Christ is waiting* © 1988 WGRG from the 'Enemy of Apathy' collection.

Jubilate Hymns, 61 Chessel Avenue, Southampton SO19 4DY for *Christ triumphant, ever reigning* © Michael Saward/Jubilate Hymns, *Go forth and tell!* © Mrs. M. Seddon/Jubilate Hymns, *Let us praise God together* © Mrs M. Seddon/Jubilate Hymns, *O God beyond all praising* © Michael Perry/Jubilate Hymns, *See him lying on a bed of straw* © Michael Perry/ Jubilate Hymns, *Sing to God new songs of worship* © Michael Baughen/Jubilate Hymns and *Have you heard the raindrops?* © Christian Strover/Jubilate Hymns.

Kingsway's Thankyou Music, PO Box 75, Eastbourne, East Sussex BN23 6NW for *Abba Father, let me be* © 1977 Kingsway's Thankyou Music, *All heaven declares* © 1987 Kingsway's Thankyou Music, *All over the world* © 1984 Kingsway's Thankyou Music, *Ascribe greatness* © 1979 Peter West/Integrity's Hosanna! Music, administered by Kingsway's Thankyou Music for Europe (excl. German speaking countries), international copyright secured, all rights reserved, *Be still for the presence of the Lord* © 1986 Kingsway's Thankyou Music, *Bind us together, Lord* © 1977 Kingsway's Thankyou Music, *By your side* © 1989 Kingsway's Thankyou Music, *Colours of day* 1974 Kingsway's Thankyou Music, *Come on and celebrate* © 1984 Kingsway's Thankyou Music, *Father God, I wonder* © 1984 Kingsway's Thankyou Music, *Father, I place into your hands* © 1975 Kingsway's Thankyou Music, *For I'm building a people of power* © 1977 Kingsway's Thankyou Music, *From heaven you came* © 1983 Kingsway's Thankyou Music, *Give thanks with a grateful heart* ©1978